MAKERS
of the
MUSLIM
WORLD

Usama ibn Munqidh

"Paul Cobb has written a vibrant, comprehensive biography of Usama
ibn Munqidh, the Syrian emir whose stories, especially those relating to
Muslim-Frankish encounters, have fascinated generations of historians and
undergraduate students."

PROFESSOR BENJAMIN Z. KEDAR

MAKERS
of the
MUSLIM
WORLD

Usama ibn Munqidh

Warrior-Poet of the Age of Crusades

PAUL M. COBB

ONEWORLD

OXFORD

USAMA IBN MUNQIDH

Oneworld Publications
(Sales and editorial)
185 Banbury Road
Oxford OX2 7AR
England
www.oneworld-publications.com

ISBN 1–85168–403–4

Typeset by Sparks, Oxford, UK
Cover and text design by Design Deluxe
Printed and bound in India by Thomson Press Ltd
on acid-free paper

TO THE MEMORY OF GOLIARD BOOKSHOP
SO I WRITE — POETS — ALL —
THEIR SUMMER — LASTS A SOLID YEAR —

CONTENTS

PREFACE

> There is no heroic poem in the world but is at bottom a biography,
> the life of a man; also it may be said, there is no life of a man,
> faithfully recorded, but is a heroic poem of its sort, rhymed or
> unrhymed.
>
> Thomas Carlyle (1838)

In the summer of 1880, the French scholar Hartwig Derenbourg discovered a manuscript in a box in the Escorial Library in Madrid. In a certain sense, in that box, Derenbourg also discovered a person.

The manuscript turned out to be the sole surviving copy of a book called in Arabic *Kitab al-I'tibar*, or *The Book of Learning by Example*, usually referred to these days as the "memoirs" of a medieval Muslim warrior and poet from the period of the Crusades, Usama ibn Munqidh. Born in 1095, the year Pope Urban II proclaimed the First Crusade, and dying in 1188, just months after the Muslims recaptured Jerusalem, Usama virtually embodies the age of the Crusades. In his day a famed poet and man of letters, the son of a noble Arab family famed for its courage and courtliness, Usama lived an unusually adventurous life, serving as a commander and adviser to some of the most famous rulers of the medieval Middle East during a pivotal epoch in world history. As the great Turkish warlords faced the threat of the Crusader states in Syria, Usama was there. As the rulers of Egypt saw their empire collapse around them, Usama was there, and as the near-legendary Saladin launched his counter-crusade, Usama was there to tell us all about it in his poems and his autobiographical musings. Before Derenbourg's discovery, Usama was almost completely unknown to the world and so, in an important way, Usama is the child of his philological loins. Derenbourg was the first to note the incredible historical and cultural value of the *Book of Learning* and the first to try his hand at editing and translating this difficult and incomplete text. Moreover, he was the first to assemble as much as he could find of snippets of texts by and about Usama quoted in other medieval Arabic works. And, most importantly, he was the first to gather all this material and to attempt to stitch it all together in a chronological sequence and compose a biography (Derenbourg, *Vie*, 1889).

Some sense of this pioneering achievement can be gained when we consider that his biography of Usama weighs in at 731 pages, and that it is only the first part of a larger study containing textual editions, translations, and scholarly digressions, a totality that, I can attest, comes close to transgressing current guidelines for carry-on luggage on several major international airlines. All this in an era when the vast majority of the texts were unedited and unprinted, meaning that he could consult them only in manuscript form, in scattered (and generally uncataloged) collections in Europe and the Middle East. In short, without Derenbourg's genetic exertions, there would be no Usama as we know him today.

While better editions and better translations have replaced Derenbourg's, his biography of Usama remains a monument of nineteenth-century scholarship on the medieval Islamic world. This little book in no way attempts to alter that. Rather, it aims to add a level, by offering, in English, a short and readable biography that is intended to be accessible to the non-specialist as well as to present a bird's-eye view of the world in which Usama lived and to assess the degree to which he can be said to have contributed to it. Was Usama, for all his political and literary feats, really a "Maker of the Muslim World?" That is the question that this slim biography will address. If this book advances a point here or there at the expense of previous scholarship, then this is thanks solely to the existence of definitive edited texts, some of them unknown to Derenbourg, and to a further century of scholarship on the medieval Islamic world. Finally, if this book should encourage interested readers to learn more about the medieval Middle East and the history and literature that both Usama and Derenbourg loved, then I will be doubly gratified.

What this book does that Derenbourg was not able to do is to take into account much of Usama's literary output that was either unknown or unavailable in the 1880s, including his poetry anthology and many other works that are of biographical and literary interest (see list below). Thanks to Derenbourg, and to Philip Hitti's very popular English translation of Usama's "memoirs," Usama has become famous as a Muslim observer of the Franks, and, to some, as a warrior and model of medieval Islamic chivalry. But he was known to his peers primarily as a man of letters, and it is this aspect of Usama's life that I have tried to reaffirm in this book. The texts by and about Usama that have come to light since Derenbourg's time have been especially useful in this regard. Although this book is thus intended for first-time visitors to medieval Islamic history, I hope specialists may find in it a few things that are new to them.

A note about citation: in an attempt to make this life of a medieval Muslim as accessible as possible, I have not cluttered the text with citations, except when identifying quotations or possibly contentious statements, when I include short citations to the sources in parentheses. The bibliography at the end of the book thus represents only those works cited in the text, not the many other works I consulted. In keeping with the goals of this series, I also include some suggestions for further reading. In this book, all translations are my own, with the exception of quotations from Usama's "memoirs," which are those of Hitti, often with some slight emendations. Where applicable, I cite sources using the page number of the edited medieval text (Arabic, Latin, or Syriac) followed by the page number of any existing translation, separated by a "/". When citing Usama's own works, I use the following abbreviations (asterisk indicates a text unknown to Derenbourg):

KI *Kitab al-I'tibar*, Hitti ed., Princeton, 1930.
*LA *Lubab al-Adab*, Shakir ed., Cairo, 1935.
KA *Kitab al-'Asa*, 'Abbas ed., Alexandria, 1978.
*BB *Al-Badi' fi'l-badi'*, Muhanna ed., Beirut, 1987. Derenbourg was made aware of the text as he was finishing his *Vie*; he provides a summary of its contents in an appendix.
*MD *Kitab al-Manazil wa'l-Diyar*, Hijazi ed., Cairo, 1968.
*Diwan *Diwan Usama ibn Munqidh*, Badawi & 'Abd al-Majid eds., Cairo, 1953.

Manaqib Manaqib 'Umar ibn al-Khattab wa-Manaqib 'Umar
ibn 'Abd al-'Aziz, Dar al-Kutub, Cairo: MS *ta'rikh* Taymur
#1513 (11147). Derenbourg used a folio as a frontispiece for his
Vie but did not examine the work in detail.

My hope is that, by doing without footnotes and the usual dry style
of high scholarship, I have produced something for people who might
otherwise avoid a book about someone as interesting as Usama; yet
also something that the specialists can learn to enjoy.

A few quick words about some editorial matters: medieval Islamic
names can be daunting and confusing even for specialists. A medieval Muslim, particularly a medieval aristocrat like Usama, might
be known by any number of names or titles or their combinations.
Technically, Usama was "Majd al-Din Usama ibn Murshid ibn 'Ali
ibn Munqidh al-Kinani." Let's break that up into its components:
"Majd al-Din" was a fancy title meaning "The Glory of Religion," but
it didn't mean that Usama was particularly religious or glorious, as
everyone bore such epithets in his day. "Usama" is his given name;
"ibn" means "son of" ("bint" in women's names means "daughter
of") and "Murshid" was his father's given name. Genealogy was very
important to the medieval Arabs; and this is reflected in their names,
which extend back many generations, linked by "ibns" and "bints." So,
although it is common to refer to Usama as "Usama ibn Munqidh,"
in honor of Munqidh, the founder of his clan, he is properly Usama
ibn Murshid, "Usama, the son of Murshid." Finally, "al-Kinani" is an
adjective indicating that Usama (and his kinsmen) came from the
Kinana tribe.

Additionally, people might be known by an array of nicknames.
Men, most typically, were known by the name of their eldest male
child, as "Father of so-and-so." Thus, Usama, whose eldest son was
called Murhaf, was also known as "Father of Murhaf," in Arabic, Abu
Murhaf ("Abu" meaning father; in women's names, "Umm" means
mother). And, as with English names like Rex or Don, sometimes
names look like titles. Usama's uncle, for example, had the given
name "Sultan," but he was not a sultan by trade. But such cases are
rare.

In the medieval texts upon which this biography is based, one encounters every kind of naming technique. To simplify things for my readers, I have "silently regularized" personal names, by choosing one form of the name and staying with it, even though this has sometimes involved a little awkwardness in English and an unnatural dose of pronouns. To assist matters, I have included a list of principal people encountered in this book (see p. 125ff.) with quick identifying descriptions.

I have avoided the usual but terrifying dots and dashes and special symbols used to transliterate non-Latin alphabets like Arabic into the Latin alphabet in the hope that specialists won't need the symbols and non-specialists won't miss them. Accordingly, if a commonly accepted English version of a name or term exists, I have used it. Thus, I use Mecca, not the scholarly form Makka, and Saladin, not Salah al-Din.

All dates in this book are Common Era, having usually been converted from dates given according to the Islamic calendar in the medieval sources. As such, there is always a slight degree of uncertainty with regard to chronology, but no more than a factor of one day.

Even a book as small as this has, nevertheless, a big debt to pay. It was written contemporaneously with a larger forthcoming history of Usama's clan, the Banu Munqidh. All the people and institutions that have guided and assisted me in my various descents into Munqidhiana over the past few years will be acknowledged in that study, so any absences here will be remedied. However, some of those people have been so helpful with this book that they deserve double exposure, though they are not responsible for any of the flaws that remain. For all the support and goodwill granted during the research and writing of this book, I would first like to thank my colleagues in the Department of History and the Medieval Institute at the University of Notre Dame. Patricia Crone kindly offered the opportunity to write this book for her series, and she and the anonymous reader kept me on the straight and narrow. The people at Oneworld Publications have been a joy to work with, particularly Mark Hopwood, Victoria Roddam, and Ann Grand. The map of the

Near East c. 1150 is based upon a map produced by Mr. Don Pirius of DP Cartographic Services. The photo of Shayzar Castle on p. 2 is used with kind permission of Christina Tonghini.

I gambled with the friendship of Don-John Dugas, John Iskander and John Meloy by asking them to read a draft of this book before it deserved reading. Their comments saved me much embarrassment, and I hope I have not lost the gamble as a result.

In Egypt, I would like to thank Taef El-Azhari, Mandy McClure, Amgad Naguib, and Ahmed Selim. In Syria and Lebanon, I must thank Georges Baroud, Antoine Borrut, Nadia El-Cheikh, Clare Leader, John Meloy, and Anne Troadec. Others provided help divorced from any merely geographical context: Niall Christie, L. M. Harteker, R. Stephen Humphreys, Georgio Meloy, Carl Petry, Megan Reid, Cristina Tonghini, Paul Walker, and the Cobb family, who have happily encouraged me to write a book that they would actually read.

I first figured out what poetry was at the now-defunct Goliard Bookshop of Amherst, Massachusetts, even though I'd been reading it for years. I dedicate this book to its memory.

INTRODUCTION

THE WORLD OF USAMA IBN MUNQIDH

The world of Usama ibn Munqidh was a fragmented world. Once upon a time, the Middle East was, at least superficially, politically unified. After the great Islamic conquests of the seventh century, the lands from Spain to Central Asia were ruled by *caliphs*. Caliphs – the word connotes succession or place-holding – were men recognized as suitable political successors of the Prophet Muhammad (d. 632), and it was they who shepherded the political union that he had formed at Islam's birth into the more complicated times of later centuries. Although, under the Umayyad dynasty, the caliphate had been based in Syria, after 750 it was held by the Abbasid dynasty, who made Iraq their home and Baghdad their capital. From Iraq, the Abbasid caliphs controlled one of the most powerful early medieval empires, whose reputation spread far and wide.

By Usama's day all that was long gone. Centuries before he was born in Syria in 1095, the fragile unity of the Abbasid caliphate had been shattered. With telling speed, province after province broke away from the authority of the caliphs. Some provinces symbolically recognized their suzerainty but in practice acted autonomously. In Usama's day, an Abbasid caliph still sat in Baghdad, but he had little real authority beyond his own palace. In Iraq, power devolved to the Abbasid military and the men who controlled it. And elsewhere in the lands of Islam, men of different sorts, from petty warlords to rival caliphs, laid claim to their own fluctuating domains.

Being fragmented, the world Usama inhabited was one where unity and unification were common preoccupations. In the eleventh century, the political powers of most consequence in the Middle

East were the Saljuq sultans, usually based either in Iran or in Iraq, and their rivals, the Fatimid caliphs of Egypt. The Fatimids were a Shiʿite dynasty who bitterly sought the final end of the Abbasids, whom they regarded as usurpers of the Prophet's patrimony. The Saljuqs, on the other hand, were Sunnis – the cliché is to call them "staunch" Sunnis – who saw themselves as protectors of the Abbasid dynasty and a bulwark of Sunnism against Shiʿites and other groups deemed heretical. Unlike the Fatimids, the Saljuq ruling class was Turkish in origin, having been part of the massive migrations of Turkish nomads into Iran, Iraq and Anatolia ("Turkey") that took place over the eleventh century. Both Fatimids and Saljuqs were, at least theoretically, intent on unifying the Islamic world under their aegis, dreaming of reviving or indeed surpassing the glory and might of the old Abbasid caliphate.

As chance would have it, Syria was precisely where the frontiers of these rival powers met and so it could resist being swallowed up by either the Saljuqs or the Fatimids. When one considers that the Byzantine Empire, Syria's Greek-speaking, Christian neighbor to the north, also laid claim to territory in the region, one can appreciate the political opportunities available. Local rulers and men of influence could survive simply by playing the two (or three) powers off each other. Unlike regions under direct Saljuq or Fatimid control, Syria had an unusual number of local rulers who retained a good measure of independence or semi-independence, at times working as servants of the Fatimids, at times as servants of the Saljuqs, and at other times ignoring both. This seemed to be contagious, for even when the Fatimids or Saljuqs sent loyal servants to Syria as governors or commanders, the fluctuating political currents of that province often encouraged a rebellious sense of independent thinking.

The men who served the sultans, helping them govern their empire, were military men, known by various titles. Any man who had troops following him, or the requisite social standing, was an *amir* (sometimes spelled "emir"), a word used today for Arab princes (and reflected in "The United Arab Emirates"), but which, in Usama's time, merely meant "commander." The Saljuqs liked to give their princes training in government and statecraft before they became sultans in their own right, and so they customarily served as governors of provinces in their family's domains. But often they were sent as children, and so a particularly trustworthy or skilful commander went with them. These men were called *atabegs*. Atabegs were expected to serve their charges as commanders of their army and as tutors and companions. As trustworthy as some might be, there were some bad apples, and it was quite common for atabegs to usurp their young charges and rule in their place. In distant places, like Usama's Syria, the possibility that independently minded atabegs might break away completely was never far away.

To help them govern, amirs and atabegs had large armies of horse-men and infantry, usually of Turkish, Arab, or Kurdish origin, and often containing men who were *mamluks*, that is, of servile origin. Typically, these were enslaved prisoners of war who had been freed by their commanders and trained as their soldiers. Commanders and the soldiers under them were rewarded with *iatq's*: cash stipends and assignments of lands (or the responsibility to collect taxes from lands). Despite the great diversity in their use, iatq's in Usama's day resembled medieval European fiefs (but of course they differed from them, too). Well-rewarded amirs got farms or villages as iatq's; *very* well-rewarded amirs got whole provinces. With these men and these tools, the Saljuq sultans tried to unify Usama's fragmented world.

Among the petty regional rulers in Syria who still clung to their autonomy, despite Saljuq and Fatimid attempts to discourage them, were the Banu Munqidh, Usama's family. Through political savvy, military skill, and the strategic use of cold, hard cash, the Banu Munqidh made themselves a force to be reckoned with in eleventh-century Syria, fending and buying off Byzantine, Fatimid, Saljuq, and other local aggressors. Centered on the citadel of their castle at Shayzar (see map page xxiii), the family domains fluctuated over the decades, but the core of their authority was the area from Shayzar to the banks of the Orontes river, westward to the Jabal Ansariya moun-tains, and eastward into the Jabal al-Summaq region with the small fortified towns of Apamea, Kafartab, and Ma'arrat al-Nu'man. For purely geographical reasons, the Banu Munqidh were more closely involved in the courts of the Saljuq governors in Aleppo than in those of their counterparts in Damascus. In the politics of northern Syria, the Banu Munqidh were not to be ignored. Nor were they strangers to the courts of other Saljuq potentates in Iraq or Iran; and one branch of the family even lived in Cairo.

In 1098, a new element was added to this mix of regional powers and petty princes: the European Crusaders. These interlopers were known to the Arabic sources simply as "the Franks," despite their varied origins. After entering into a tenuous alliance with the Byzantine emperor in 1097, the Crusaders had crossed into Anatolia, and, by June of 1098 had captured Antioch. This city, once a center of early Christianity, was henceforth the center of one of the few long-lasting Crusader principalities in the region. After Antioch, one of the first places the Franks encountered on their embattled road to Jerusalem was Shayzar, where the Banu Munqidh, ever sensitive to political realities, assisted the Crusaders to cross the Orontes river and get out of their territories as quickly as possible. Around the cities of Edessa, Tripoli, and, of course, Jerusalem, other Crusader states were carved out of Muslim territory. Nevertheless, the Franks that remained in the principality of Antioch would be a frequent thorn in the side of Shayzar, and would shape Usama's earliest impressions of the Franks.

Usama's world was predominantly, but not exclusively, Muslim. This was particularly true of the ruling elites, all of whom, except the Frankish rulers of the Crusader states, were Muslims. It was rather less true of the rest of the population: in Syria and Egypt of the eleventh century, Muslims had only recently become a majority. Syria, Iraq, and especially Egypt had significant Christian communities of various kinds, and Jewish communities had deep roots in the region, particularly in major urban centers like Baghdad, Damascus, and, above all, Cairo. Other smaller communities, such as the Samaritans of Palestine or the Druze of central Syria, added to the region's religious diversity.

While the struggle between the regional powers of the Fatimids and the Saljuqs could at times heighten tensions between ordinary Sunnis and Shi'ites, Muslims from both groups, and from the subsects within them, tended to live comfortably alongside one another and alongside non-Muslim communities. This was largely because Islamic law accorded, to Jews and Christians at least, a protected social and political status, *dhimma*, and so they were called *dhimmis*. Bigotry was never absent, but as long as dhimmis paid a certain tax and kept their place, as fellow monotheists or "Peoples of the Book," they could practice their religion freely and be valued subjects of the empire, not to mention employees or neighbors. As for Sunnis and Shi'ites, centuries of coexistence in Syria had familiarized both camps with one another, and, while there was certainly tension, among normal folk such religious differences tended not to matter much.

There are three glaring exceptions to this general rule of grudging coexistence that the reader will encounter in histories of this period: first, the Crusaders' assaults on native Muslim, Jewish, and Christian populations (that is, those who did not surrender to Frankish rule); second, the occasional massacre of non-Muslims by Muslims as the Muslim reaction to the Crusader threat became more shrill; and third, the politico-religious divisions and rivalries within the variety of Shi'ism practiced by the Fatimid ruling elite, called Isma'ili Shi'ism. One such Isma'ili sect, the Nizaris – vulgarly known as the Assassins – could be famously uncompromising toward fellow Shi'ites as well as to Sunnis and others. Their attacks against perceived obstacles to their expansion in Syria reached their height in Usama's lifetime.

Complex as the religious map of the medieval Middle East was, it was further complicated by the region's ethnic diversity. The people that Usama encountered on a daily basis would be recognized today as Arabs, Turks, Persians, Kurds, Armenians, Europeans, and Africans, to name only the largest ethnic groups. Usama's world was rich with cultural nuances. For members of the ruling elite, whatever their background, cultural expression was most strongly marked by the impulses of the religion of Islam, the language of Arabic, and the customs and practices of the Arabic-speaking populations of the region, with occasional signs of influences from the Turco-Persian realm favored by the Saljuq elite. As Usama himself famously came to appreciate, his own culture – the monotheist, patriarchal, agricultural, equestrian civilization of the elite – even found some admirers among the region's Frankish settlers, who came from not dissimilar cultural realms.

Usama's writings leave little doubt that, for him at least, and for many other Muslims, rigid adherence to the letter of Islamic law was laudable, but rarely pursued. Indeed, Islam explicitly features little in Usama's writings but provides an over-arching framework within which he (and others) structured their relationship to God. Certainly this relationship was shaped by the injunctions of the Qur'an and Islamic law, but also by Islamic mystical and ascetical practices that tend to be lumped together as "Sufism." For Usama, organized Sufi brotherhoods were a novelty; although asceticism and Sufism had been around for centuries, he did not encounter any until relatively late in his life. Far more common were the less organized and less institutional devotional expressions of personal piety: fasting, praying, giving alms, reciting and copying the Qur'an and so on. To this list should also be added the visitation of tombs of holy men, a cultural practice that Usama engaged in and commented upon several times in his writings.

This discussion of "culture" would have puzzled Usama; for him and other literate inhabitants of his world, true culture was summed up in the concept of *adab*, a complex of genteel ways and manners, artful facility with language and wit, and razor-honed skills in poetry and rhetoric. In addition, any proper gentleman, such as Usama, would be expected to know the arts of war and its adjunct, the hunt. Medicine, mathematics and the "harder" sciences tended to be left to the specialists, but even mathematicians who wanted to make it big were supposed, as befitting their social setting, to know a little poetry or possess a modicum of *adab*. That said, it was not unknown for cultured men to dabble in things scientific, and Usama frequently purveys bits of medical advice in his writings. *Adab* was not just the purview of poets, but of anyone with pretensions to culture. As it happens, Usama was a great theoretician of this culture and was lionized by his contemporaries for embodying the *adab* of his age.

Any socially well-placed man was thus expected to be able to demonstrate his superiority over his enemies, over his social peers, and over nature. It was also the working assumption of the day that the affairs of men took precedence over those of women, who were most commonly regarded as pillars of the family, and thus society, and whose chastity men were obliged to police rigorously. In Usama's time, the domestic seclusion of women, especially elite women, was the norm, so much so that medieval Muslim authors have left us very little information about women's private lives. It is thus all the more surprising to see that Usama has left us a number of precious, but discreet, glimpses into this part of his world.

The fissures of Usama's fragmented world were spanned by a supportive cultural unity, a common bridge of patriarchy, God-fear, horsemanship and *adab* with which even intruders like the Franks could find affinities. One can grasp some sense of the nature of the achievement of medieval Islamic civilization in this regard when one considers that this relative unity was achieved amidst great ethnic and religious diversity, and despite great topographical obstacles. Like any other vast area, the Middle East has never been given to unities. And recall that Usama lived most of his life in lands that were frontier areas to the power regions of Iraq, Iran and Egypt. Syria was traversed by mountain ranges, river valleys, and deserts, which made political unification, as well as cultural uniformity, a real challenge.

Shayzar, Usama's home, was in the Orontes valley, just beyond the north-western limit of the Syrian desert, a vast and rugged plain that extends northward from its parent steppe in the Arabian Peninsula. The desert's eastern margins are truncated by the Euphrates river-valley, with the fragment to the east of the river forming the Jazira, the fertile plain of northern Iraq. To the west, the Syrian desert is almost continuously interrupted from north to south by a double defense against the Mediterranean Sea. This defense comes first from the northern extension of the east African Rift Valley, known by different names within Syria, but comprising the Gulf of 'Aqaba, the Dead Sea, the Jordan Valley, the Sea of Galilee, the Beqaa Valley, and the Orontes Valley. The water sources, agriculture, and trade routes that congregate along this seam became, from very early times, the foci for human settlement, and by the time Usama entered the picture, the inland cities of Jerusalem, Damascus, Aleppo, and many others were very ancient indeed. The desert's second line of defense is formed by a line of rugged hills that increase in altitude and isolation from south to north, from the relatively tame Palestinian hills to the sharp and snow-capped mountains of Lebanon and the Amanus Range in the north. At some locations, the mountains loom perilously over the Mediterranean Sea, leaving only a thin, but fertile, coastal strip. This band along the eastern Mediterranean coast has thus naturally been the chosen site for rich and thriving port cities with pedigrees as venerable as any interior city: Acre, Tripoli, Beirut, and many others.

If there is any geographical key to appreciating Usama's life, then it is to be sought in Shayzar, in the castle, the town, and the countryside around. This is where Usama learned his most valuable life lessons, and which, throughout his long exile, teasingly beckoned to him, symbolizing the restfulness and autonomy he never managed to attain.

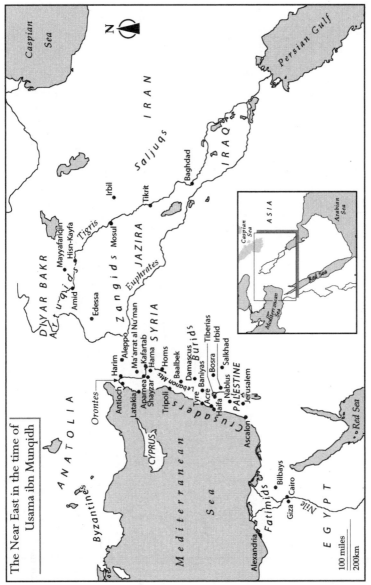

The Near East in the time of
Usama ibn Munqidh

Map by **MAP**grafix

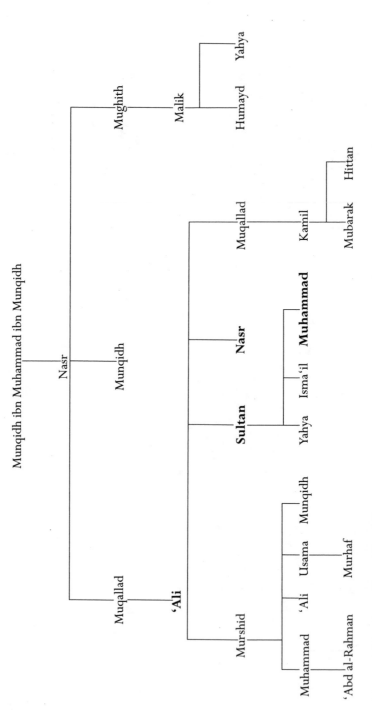

Figure 1 The Banu Munqidh of Shayzar

1

THE YOUTH AND THE CASTLE

On July 4, 1095, Usama ibn Munqidh entered his world just as we all did ours: with limited horizons that expanded with each passing hour, day, month, and year. A room in a maze of rooms deep in a castle; a castle perched over a town; a town linked to other towns through roads, hunting paths, and a host of human relationships. These were the settings that defined Usama's early life and where his earliest formative experiences took place. For all that in later life he was famed as a battle-scarred, road-weary veteran, we do well to remember that, for his first thirty or so years, he never really strayed far from the room where he was born.

THE SETTING OF SHAYZAR

Shayzar lay at the center of Usama's earlier, smaller world. Shayzar Castle, the home of Usama and his clan, the Banu Munqidh, sits imperiously atop a high and nearly inaccessible promontory of rock that extends from the surrounding plateau; a cragged northward-gesturing spear point that the local population called "The Rooster's Comb" because of its notched profile. This rock is protected on almost three sides by the Orontes river, which churns along its base to the north and east; to the south, a moat separates the rock from its parent plateau, leaving the castle almost isolated from the country surrounding it, save for its western approach. There, spreading from the western flank of the rock and north toward the river, the

1

lower town of Shayzar stood, and still stands today. For the inhabitants of Shayzar town, the castle high overhead served both as the residence of their lords, the Banu Munqidh, and as a citadel and refuge in war.

Hewn out of the white, grey, and honey-colored stone of the Orontes valley, the remaining ruins of Shayzar Castle are a monument to what we do not know. The castle ruins that visitors see today are the remains of a structure, or structures, built many years after Usama ibn Munqidh and his family passed from history. While it is more than likely that the present ruins closely approximate the castle that Usama lived in, we cannot really be certain. For Usama's family castle met a sudden and bitter end, and lies largely hidden. The present ruins thus provide a general sense of Usama's home, but we need the medieval sources to flesh out some of the details.

Just as one enters the ruins in the present day, in Usama's day one could only approach Shayzar castle from the town, along a ramp that stretched to the castle's northern (and, apparently, only) gate. From a dark, enclosed, probably dog-legged passageway, one entered a hall and then stepped – blinking, presumably – into the castle grounds. The castle stretched axially from its northern gate straight to the southern tip of the rock, and then, as now, ended in an imposing defensive tower. Sources describe families in the Banu Munqidh household as having individual residences, some with towers, some

Shayzar Castle, view from the north

with winding stairs and windows. These homes were, almost certainly, of standard mud-brick and stone, with rooms grouped around a courtyard where, we are told, arched porticos provided shade. Save for a dungeon, some stables mentioned in passing, and (to judge by the current ruins), some wells or cisterns, these are the main reliable details of what Shayzar looked like in Usama's day. If, as seems likely, Usama's Shayzar was built at least partly of the stones in the present ruins, then we can appreciate, in the near-constant breeze, how cool the interiors would have been on a summer afternoon, how positively cold and dank in wet weather, and how, at sunset on clear days, Shayzar Castle would flame brightly as the town below slipped into darkness.

The sounds of Shayzar would have been telling. Usama grew up amidst the rhythms of a medieval town; the hammering and pounding of myriad tasks and arts, the crunch of gravel, and the crackle of hearths. Animals, and their calls, were everywhere: bleating herds of sheep and goats being driven to pasture, discernible far away, braying donkeys objecting to their labors, whickering horses, dogs snoring, a hunting falcon screeching its challenge to its prey, and, just maybe, a lion roaring in the distant hills. And always, ever-present, the river. The Orontes lapped at the foot of Shayzar and gurgled past on its northward course; in the dry summer months exposed rocky patches could serve as fords for those who knew the river, and after rains and the spring thaw, the river slowly churned at full crest, making crossing impossible save by the town's sole bridge, and leaving marshy areas, where waterfowl congregated, just outside the town. As long as the river obliged, it also added one last sonic dimension to life at Shayzar: the measured, incessant groaning of mills located on the river's banks and islands up and down the valley. Some of these milled grain; others propelled water into the town and across the fields. Today, in the nearby city of Hama, grander, much noisier descendants of these traditional Syrian mills can still be seen, and heard.

By proving itself an obstacle, the river also proved a boon to Shayzar. Local knowledge notwithstanding, a person could generally only cross the river by a nearby bridge. Moreover, only one road served this bridge, and it ran right through Shayzar and under the watchful gaze of the Banu Munqidh. The ford at Shayzar was one of the few crossing points in the region, and it was guarded jealously. Control of the ford meant control of Shayzar. Even before they had come into possession of Shayzar, the Banu Munqidh had built a fortress at the bridge, and, after moving to Shayzar, stationed a small body of soldiers there to prevent enemies from crossing unopposed. From the bridge, the Banu Munqidh could travel to other lands of their small principality: scattered fields and outlying villages, but also, at times, fortresses and towns as far away as Latakia on the coast, or Kafartab on the road to Aleppo.

By 1095, the year Usama was born, the Banu Munqidh had been lords of Shayzar for fifteen years, having captured it from the Byzantines in 1080. But the family had been moderately influential in northern Syrian affairs for generations, particularly in the courts of Tripoli and Aleppo. By the time they captured Shayzar, the Banu Munqidh were a recognized family of power, with a reputation, even in distant Cairo, for honor, courtliness, and soldiering. At Usama's birth, his uncle Nasr was the head of the household, but his other uncle, Sultan, and his father, Murshid, played increasingly important roles in maintaining the affairs of the principality. Indeed, in the months prior to Usama's birth, Murshid was away on a mission in Iran, petitioning the Saljuq sultan for the return of some of the family lands. His business in the court completed, Murshid arrived back in Shayzar just in time for the birth of the second of his four sons. He named him Usama, "lion," a prescient gesture, given that the boy would become famous as a hunter of his leonine namesake.

Upon Usama's uncle Nasr's death in 1098, the succession to the lordship of Shayzar became a matter of family controversy. In the end, unexpectedly, Usama's uncle Sultan, not his father Murshid, became the new lord of Shayzar in 1098. Murshid was certainly the elder of the two brothers, but he appears to have had serious misgivings about becoming a full-time politician. He was noted for his piety, and this, according to the sources, was the reason behind his singular decision upon Nasr's death: he refused the succession as a worldly distraction and let it pass to Sultan. "No, by God," some sources have him swearing, "I will not enter into the affairs of this world!" Murshid remained by his brother Sultan's side, but henceforth Sultan was lord of Shayzar. From that position, he would have a decisive impact on Usama's future (Ibn 'Asakir, *Ta'rikh*, 1998, 57: 216).

CHILDHOOD

Usama had no formal education, in the sense that we would recognize it today. For a son of the rural aristocracy like Usama, education more commonly came through tutors and kinsmen. Usama's father had been tutored to memorize the Qur'an, and he considered the study of scripture to be an act of pious merit that went beyond the common day-to-day gestures of Muslim religiosity. Indeed, Usama tells us that, alongside hunting, the study of the Qur'an was Murshid's chief occupation in life. By the time he died, he had personally produced over forty copies of the Qur'an, many lavishly decorated, as well as an immense commentary on it and its style, grammar, and various readings. It is no surprise that he encouraged all his children to be on intimate terms with the Qur'an, its lessons, its languages, and its rhythms. And, given Usama's social context, it was perfectly natural that this learning should go on in the midst of his other daily activities, on the hunt if necessary (KI, 201 / 230):

> On the day on which [my father] would start for the mountain to hunt partridges, while he was en route towards the mountain but still at some distance from it, he would say to us, "Disperse. Every one of you who has not yet recited his assignment in the Qur'an will do it now." We, his children, knew the Qur'an by heart. We would then disperse and recite our assignments until we got to the hunting field. He would thereupon order someone to summon us and would question each one of us as to how much we had read.

In other matters of the spirit, Murshid was less successful in guiding his son. Like many Muslims of his day, Usama's father knew that he lived as part of some unknowable divine plan, and that some of the possible vectors of that plan could be observed in the movements of the stars and planets. Medieval Islamic study of the heavens combined astronomy and astrology in the modern sense, in that, while based upon "scientific" observation of the night skies and their denizens, its purpose was, for Usama's father and many others like him, directed at plumbing even deeper mysteries. But for every devotee of the stars, there was a skeptic. Despite his urging, Usama never really took to this aspect of his father's world, seeing in it a strange contradiction to his other pious pursuits. However, at Shayzar, on clear summer nights, it would be surprising if he did not turn heavenward and wonder quietly about the ineffable; later, Usama would fondly remember how the old man would point out the stars and tell him their names (KI, 56/85).

For areas requiring more technical guidance, Murshid, like many other men of his standing, employed professional tutors to educate his children. Tutoring in medieval Syria was rather like the practice known to the ancient Greeks and Romans. Tutors were not professional teachers, but scholars who, in order to make a living, sought residence and patronage in a suitable household as a tutor or copyist. Physicians were in much the same situation. For them, attachment to a household provided the means (and the media) for their work. This being so, there could be significant difficulty in attracting decent tutors in smaller households like Shayzar, for the best scholars were attracted to wealthy urban courts. However, in Usama's childhood, thanks to the disruptions and dislocations of the Turkish invasions and the Crusades, it was essentially a buyer's market for tutors, and one gets the sense that a flurry of scholars, poets, and physicians, most of them unnamed, made their way through Shayzar.

For example, a locally renowned Syrian poet and man of letters, Ibn Munira, appears as Usama's tutor, and it is surely relevant that he was from Kafartab, a town that the Banu Munqidh had once controlled but which, after 1098, found itself in Frankish hands. Ibn Munira was a retiring character, and although Usama once impishly suggested that even he should don armor and fight the Franks, the scholar replied that he was a man of reason and, since all reason left a man in combat, he would certainly do no such thing. Another tutor was in a similar situation: Abu 'Abdallah al-Tulaytuli, born in Toledo in Spain, was hailed by Usama as one of the greatest grammarians of his age. He had once worked as the chief scholar in the academy of the Syrian port of Tripoli, a city that attracted scholars, copyists, and books from diverse regions. When the Franks captured it in 1109, Usama's father and uncle rescued Abu 'Abdallah, and took him into their service at Shayzar. Usama studied grammar with him for nearly a decade in his late teens and early twenties. He later recounted an anecdote about this teacher, describing a situation familiar to any academic visited by students. One day, Usama went to his tutor's chamber to study grammar with him and found him sitting with all the principal books on the subject lying before him. Impressed by this material manifestation of his tutor's learning, the young student asked him, "Shaykh Abu 'Abdallah, have you read *all* these books?" "Read them?" the tutor replied coolly, "No, by God, I have rather inscribed them on the tablet [of my heart] and memorized them all." He then went on to prove it by having Usama select a line at random, from which point he finished the page by heart (KI, 208–209/238).

Despite this exposure to high-quality book-learning, the young Usama acquired most of his education in the school of hard knocks, that is, from the everyday examples, guidance, and chastisement of family members. At Shayzar, he was surrounded by family (see figure 1). His father Murshid and his uncle Sultan dominate his memories of his younger years. But he also had his mother, three brothers, and at least one sister and one grandmother, not to mention several uncles, a horde of cousins, the wives of his male kin, and the servants of the various households, many of whom he loved and respected deeply. In all these people, he saw, as he grew older, life's lessons displayed in three areas in particular: the hunt, warfare, and that universal human pastime, observing others.

HUNTING AT SHAYZAR

Hunting in medieval Syria, or at least the kind of hunting practiced at Shayzar, was very much like its medieval European counterpart.

Although people from the lower strata of society pursued game as a matter of course and indeed as a matter of survival, the chase was, above all, a pastime of the elite and of men. For avid hunters like Usama's kin, game was pursued by land and air. On land, nets and traps were common, but proud hunters preferred to kill their game with bows and spears. From the air, hunters had allies in trained raptors such as falcons, sakers, and hawks and the like that might snatch small game like partridges on the run, scout out bigger game from on high or blind and harass them while waiting for the horsemen to arrive to finish the job. Men considered the chase on horseback through wild terrain the finest diversion. To assist them, medieval Syrian hunters made use of domesticated carnivores, usually hounds (such as the famous saluki), or, in one notable case at Shayzar, a tamed cheetah; lynxes are also recorded. Noble hunters pursued noble beasts: gazelles, antelopes, and panthers. But, whenever possible, the Banu Munqidh hunted lions — in marshes, caves, and forests, mounted, on foot, alone or in groups.

The visitor at Shayzar today may well find such pursuits impossible to fathom, the local ecosystem is so drastically changed. There are no antelopes at Shayzar today; still less would one expect cheetahs or lions. But nine hundred years ago northern Syria was a different place. Usama's Shayzar was lush, green and forested, more like the flanks of the nearby Jabal Ansariya than the nearly barren hills that stand today. If one combines the fauna of the east African savannah with the flora of Lebanon, then one is not too far from an image of medieval Shayzar's setting. And in Usama's time humans, for all their strutting about, were thin on the ground, a decided minority. The human population of Shayzar lived in close contact with serpents, lions, leopards, cheetahs, hyenas, songbirds, wild poultry, waterfowl, birds of prey, cats, dogs, gazelles, wild asses, wild boar, and hares — to name only a few of the species mentioned by Usama in his tales of hunting escapades.

In such a setting, running such game to ground, Usama learned youthful lessons about the world and the humans in it. The hunt was not just about showing an artful mastery over nature, it was also a venue in which to prove one's quality and skill in the controlled violence that was also brought to bear in war. For example, in the midst of a section devoted to exemplary behavior in battle, Usama includes an anecdote about a Shayzari soldier who, startled in the midst of a hunt, had the presence of mind to keep an attacking lion occupied with his well-padded leg until help arrived (KI, 86–87/116). As a child, Usama displayed his own courage, in the presence of his father, by killing a serpent with a knife even as it wound itself around his arm (KI, 103–104/134). He was also a keen observer of lions, noting their persistence in attack (KI, 104/135), their danger when injured, and their set ways. On the hunt, his uncle and father were constant presences, guiding and haranguing him on his technique.

Usama and his clan had two favored hunting grounds. One, for partridges and hares, was in the mountainous land south of town. Typically, when the hunters arrived there, Usama's father (KI, 201–202/230–31):

> …would order his attendants to disperse and some of them to join the falconers. In whatever direction the partridge took the air, there was sure to be in that spot a falcon ready to be flown at it. His accompanying *mamluks* and comrades, forty mounted men in all … were sure to get any bird that rose or any hare or gazelle that was started. We would reach the top of the mountain in our chase, remaining there until the late afternoon. Then we would return, after we had fed the falcons and allowed them to drink and bathe themselves in the mountain pools, arriving in town at dusk.

The other grounds, for waterfowl, francolins, hares, and gazelles, were located along the banks of the river in the marshy reedbeds west of town. Usama considered these grounds the finest of all, calling the days when they hunted in them "carefree." Typically, they would mount horses and start from the gate of Shayzar town, bringing cheetahs to help them track from the ground, and sakers and falcons from the air (KI, 202/231):

> The cheetahs and sakers would be kept outside the field while we would go into the canebrakes with the falcons … If a hare jumped, we would throw off a falcon upon it. If the falcon seized it, well and

good; otherwise as soon as the hare got beyond the canebrakes, the cheetahs would be loosed upon it. If a gazelle was started, it was allowed to run until it got beyond the brake, when a cheetah would be loosed upon it; if the cheetah seized it, well and good; otherwise the sakers would be thrown off upon it. Thus hardly a single specimen of game could escape us unless by a special dispensation of fate.

While the young Usama was thus engaged in testing the fate of the local population of game animals, he was also gaining knowledge of, and an aesthetic appreciation for, nature. Usama had his favorite haunts along the river, where he often retired after the hunt to quietly watch the local fishermen catch fish with long reed spears (KI, 219/247). He noted the medicinal properties of certain plants, observed animals in their habits and, like any hunter, stored this knowledge away. Towards the end of his days, these early experiences meant much. For an old man whose poems used the sounds and sights from these hours spent in the outdoors, these youthful days on the hunt became the source of great nostalgia, the setting for memories of days when he was as fierce as the lions he hunted and when he could watch the wild boars scuttling about the copses of liquorice trees on the shaded slopes overlooking home.

SHAYZAR'S BAD NEIGHBORS

Even had the tracking and killing of animals and the observation of nature not brought lessons of life and death home to Usama, it would hardly have mattered, for Shayzar was ideally situated to serve as a proving ground in the still bloodier context of human warfare. By the time Usama was in his early teens, the town was virtually hemmed in on all sides by potential foes. After the arrival of the Franks in northern Syria when he was an infant, Shayzar had to contend with the Frankish Principality of Antioch and the County of Tripoli primarily, although armies from Edessa and from Jerusalem were not unknown. And the Byzantine Empire had never forgotten that northern Syria had once been subject to Constantinople. Moreover, Shayzar had many Muslim foes. These most often hailed from nearby principalities like Hama or Aleppo, and Damascus could on occasion make its power felt. But the most vexing foes for Shayzar were the small, wasp-like nuisances of local lords and princelings, chief among them the Banu Munqidh's closest and most aggressive neighbor, the Muslim bandit-king, Khalaf ibn Mula'ib.

Even before Usama was born, Ibn Mula'ib had been a source of steady annoyance to the Banu Munqidh. A former associate of Usama's grandfather, Ibn Mula'ib was an Arab chieftain and lord of Homs and Apamea. He had taken to raiding the surrounding countryside and attacking his neighbors without cause. Despite a brief stint in prison in the early 1090s, he was back again after 1096 as lord of Apamea and a very bad neighbor indeed for the Banu Munqidh. He twice attacked their domains near Shayzar; Nasr, Usama's uncle, was humiliatingly defeated in an ambush, while his uncle Sultan and his father Murshid were both wounded in combat in 1104. At one point, the two neighbors seemed to have patched up their differences, and agreed to coordinate a joint attack on a nearby fortlet held by the recently arrived Franks. But Ibn Mula'ib intentionally tarried; and while the Banu Munqidh bore the brunt of the Frankish defense, he and his men stole away with their horses. Sultan returned to Shayzar full of wrath, but was to be thwarted even in vengeance: the bandit-king of Apamea fell to the daggers of Nizari assassins after an elaborately staged attack and, shortly after, Apamea became a Frankish stronghold, one perilously close to Shayzar.

Other neighbors could be equally tiresome. Usama had particular experience in conflicts with the Muslim lord of Hama, Mahmud ibn Qaraja, who often threatened Shayzar in the 1120s. But the lord of Hama was no mere bandit. He was a powerful Turkish amir recognized by the Saljuq authorities, and no easy match for the Banu Munqidh, especially when he joined forces with his brother, the lord of the nearby city of Homs. Nevertheless, the Banu Munqidh defended themselves against the frequent attacks from Hama. It was during these early confrontations that Usama observed the common horseman's sense of honor, honed his skill with the lance, and was tested by his father on his ability to keep a focused mind during battle.

The Banu Munqidh appear to have acquitted themselves well enough. Indeed, relations between Shayzar and Hama warmed sufficiently that Usama's father was happy to lend one of his most prized possessions to his neighbor, his beloved falcon, al-Yahshur. Murshid lavished rich affection on this animal and it accompanied him everywhere, even sleeping on a fur mat near its master's bed. Al-Yahshur returned these favors by being an indefatigable and loyal hunter. Every year, Usama tells us, al-Yahshur hunted with the lord of Hama for twenty days. Oddly enough, when the venerable falcon finally died at Shayzar, the lord of Hama had it sent to his city for burial, accompanied by a special funeral procession that Usama witnessed. Eventually, in 1124, the lord of Hama suggested that the Banu Munqidh, led by Usama, join him in an assault on Frankish Apamea. Unhappily for Usama, most of the fighting took place in the vast ruins of the classical city that spread beneath the medieval fortress town. Hindered by fallen columns, blocks and pits, the Muslim forces failed to dislodge their Frankish enemies and were themselves routed. The lord of Hama was himself gravely wounded by a Frankish arrow and, after a brief convalescence at Shayzar, returned to Hama, where he died.

NIZARIS ATTACK SHAYZAR

Usama's family also faced a threat still closer to home. The Nizari Isma'ili community of Syria was never in open conflict with the Banu Munqidh. Indeed, Shayzar was home to a small group of this Shi'ite sect, who had fled persecution in Aleppo. But, several years after they lost Apamea to the Franks, the Nizaris set their sights on Shayzar. Due to their small numbers, they were obliged to use craftier means of attack than the Banu Munqidh had encountered before. In March 1114, the Christian townsfolk of Shayzar celebrated their Easter festival somewhere outside the town, in one of the neighboring villages. The festival apparently did not stress religious differences overmuch, as Sultan and most of the Banu Munqidh men came down from the castle to join the celebration. With the town and the castle largely defenseless, the Nizaris decided to strike. A group of about one hundred Nizaris from Shayzar and surrounding towns rose up, expelled most of the town's remaining occupants and barred the gates. They then stormed the castle.

Meanwhile, the women and children of the Banu Munqidh household were forced to defend themselves. Usama was attending the festivities below, but his cousin Shabib had remained behind with the women, who included Usama's aunts, his uncle's wives, his sisters and others. Being one of the few male family members about, Shabib felt it was his duty to secure the safety of the household and negotiate its surrender. As Usama would later tell the tale, Shabib went out to confront the attackers and parley with their leader. The Nizaris offered to let him escape with his life and whatever property he could collect. Rather than attempt to fight them, Shabib ran back to his home and asked all the women to give him their belongings, that he might take them into safe-keeping with him. However, he was interrupted by his aunt, one of Sultan's wives, clad in chain mail and armed to the teeth. She questioned him and, appalled, dressed him down on the spot (KI, 124/153):

> What a wretched thing you are doing! You leave your uncle's daughters and the women of your family to these dogs and go away?! What kind of life would you lead, dishonored by your family, fleeing from them? Get out and fight in behalf of your family until you are killed in their midst!

Usama added that, as a result of this harangue, Shabib remained in Shayzar to fight their attackers and grew to become one of the bravest warriors of the household.

But on that day it was the women who shone in battle. Usama's mother led the defense: it was she who gathered weapons and armor and distributed them to those remaining in the castle who could fight. And it was she who sat with one of Usama's sisters on a balcony overlooking the valley of the Orontes. In this way, if any of the Nizaris should approach, she could hurl her daughter off the balcony to her death rather than allow her to lose her honor as a prisoner of heretics and the rabble. Among the other fighters in the castle was Funun, an aged female servant who had once belonged to Usama's grandfather. Veiled, she launched herself into battle against the enemy, armed with a sword, until the rest of the Banu Munqidh came to the castle's aid.

As panic spread through the castle, the expelled townspeople down below were barred from entering at the gate. They made their way to one of the castle towers, from where the women lowered ropes and hauled the men in to help in the fight. Soon enough, the Banu Munqidh themselves heard the news, rushed back to Shayzar and, after a room-by-room search, re-took their own castle. Usama participated in this melee, at one point deflecting a blow from a Nizari dagger, which left a mark on his own blade that remained to the end of his life.

For the Banu Munqidh, the Nizari assault had, quite literally, hit home. Even had they been willing to come to some understanding with the Nizaris, this attack hardened the stance of Sultan and his household. They had, through deceitful means, penetrated into the homes of the Banu Munqidh, threatened their women, children and servants, and harassed their townsfolk. The lords of Shayzar, idling at a Christian festival, were caught blind and unaware. They had been shamefully tricked and put their household at dire risk. For the Banu Munqidh, this sense of shame could only be alleviated through revenge. After securing the castle, they descended to the lower town and rounded up and killed all the Nizaris still remaining. From this point on, Usama and his kin would have no more trouble from the Nizaris of Syria.

RELATIONS WITH THE FRANKS

Sultan's chief distraction during his reign was the consolidation of the Crusader principalities in the region. Poised between the Principality of Antioch and the County of Tripoli, Shayzar could hardly avoid confrontations with the Franks. It was in one of many such confrontations that Usama gained his first experiences in warfare. Indeed, the first day in which he "saw actual fighting" was in the spring of 1110, as a boy of fourteen, when the Franks of Antioch launched a raid on Shayzar, one of their customary springtime forays into the hinterland of the town. All Usama got to see was a mild confrontation just outside the walls of the lower town, but he noted the bravery of two Kurdish warriors, and the perfidy and exaggerated caution of the Franks (KI, 65–67/94–96).

A few years later, in August of 1119, Usama confronted the Franks personally. With the Frankish troops in disarray after a singular defeat in the north of Syria, Sultan ordered him to take a small detachment of men to Apamea to pillage their fields. Usama had assumed the city would be deserted, but was disappointed. Entering the valley below the city, he and his men were surprised by a contingent of Frankish knights and footmen. They fled toward Shayzar, but, Usama tells us, at the last moment he turned about and charged his pursuers, killing one and wounding others. In fear that the tide should turn against them, the Franks fled back to Apamea. Usama returned home to assure his father that he had not been killed (KI, 40–42/67–70).

Usama had assumed he had killed one of the men he had hit, so explosive was his lance-blow, but appearances in the heat of battle, he learned, could be deceptive. Some time later, he was called to meet a visitor to Shayzar. The visitor turned out to be a Frankish knight who wanted to meet the author of the mighty but miraculously ineffective blow that had wounded his comrade. It is interesting to note that the two met as fellow professionals, not as foes. Usama and the Frankish visitor chatted not, as one might expect, about how this blow demonstrated the hardiness of the Frankish constitution or the feebleness of Usama's skills, but about how the blow had been deflected harmlessly along his ribs in such a certain way and how this surely demonstrated the inscrutability of Fate.

Another opportunity to become acquainted with the Franks occurred in June 1124. The Muslim lord of Aleppo was eager to collect the ransom for one of his most valuable prisoners, none other than Baldwin II, king of Jerusalem and regent of Antioch. In return for substantial tribute, lands, and future promises, Baldwin was released. Being experts in Frankish affairs, the Banu Munqidh were asked to arrange the details. Sultan agreed to send to Aleppo some of his own kinsmen, most likely including Usama, to act as surety for Baldwin's promises. Until proper Frankish hostages could be sent from Antioch, Baldwin remained at Shayzar as the "guest" of the Banu Munqidh. After his release, Baldwin never kept his promises to the lord of Aleppo, but he remembered well the hospitality extended to him and the hostages that replaced him. As a result, Usama tells us, the Banu Munqidh gained a certain amount of favor with their Frankish neighbors, a fact that would serve Usama well in the future (KI, 81, 103, 120/110, 133, 150).

In such confrontations, and by observing these Franks much as he did lions, the young Usama was able to learn lessons similar to those he gained on the hunt: that one man could rout an army; that a well-placed blow, however trifling, just might prove fatal; that reason and planning almost always won over rash bravery; that Franks were creatures of habit; and that, however much the Franks enjoyed using ruses in battle, they were petrified of falling victim to them. These observations, gained in war and in peace, were valuable lessons in shaping Usama as a warrior, made possible largely because of the time in which he was born, and the place where he lived his early life. They would also make his services a valuable commodity beyond Shayzar.

QUIET MOMENTS

Life at Shayzar was not all fighting and hunting. A good deal of Usama's time would have been spent helping to manage the household's lands and properties in the area, in diplomatic or social visits to neighboring principalities, or enjoying quiet diversions at home, such as a good game of chess. Usama tells us that some of Shayzar's servants whiled away the night playing chess, resting a lamp on the sleeping head of one of his father's huge hunting dogs (KI, 224–225/253). In these same years, Usama established himself as head of his own household: in 1126, he was presented with his first-born son, whom he named Murhaf. A second son, Abu Bakr, died in infancy, and we do not know when or where he was born, although

Usama once speaks of his "children" at Shayzar, implying that he had more than one while living there. Of the mother or mothers of these children, we know nothing.

The quiet, private moments at Shayzar also provided lessons. The truths of human nature were all around. Usama's father, for example, was a brave warrior and huntsman who thrived in the struggles of this world, but also a deeply pious man, ever reflecting on the next. His uncle Sultan, a fearsome and demanding lord was, none the less, terrified of mice. A constant in these years was the presence of his devoted nurse Lu'lu'a. This redoubtable woman had raised Usama's father and, as Usama related (KI, 186/217):

> When my father grew old enough, he left the house of his father, and she left with him. When I was born, that same old woman brought me up until I became old enough to marry and leave the house of my father, and she left with me. When my children were born, she brought them up. She was one of the most pious of women, who spent her days fasting and her nights at prayer.

Such people linked Usama directly to his family's past and served as affectionate reminders of the certainty of life's trajectory and the process of aging (KI, 186/218):

> I once went in to see her in an apartment which I had reserved for her use in my house and found in front of her a basin in which she was washing a cloth for use in prayer. I asked her, "What is this, mother?" She replied, "My dear son, someone has handled this cloth with hands soiled with cheese, and the more I wash it the more it stinks of cheese." I said to her, "Show me the soap with which you are washing it." She pulled out the soap from the cloth and I saw then that it was a piece of cheese which she took for soap ... Blessed be God the most truthful of speakers, who said: "He whose days we lengthen, we reverse his exterior form." (Qur'an 36:68)

Usama also greatly admired his grandmother, who generated a special sense of awe in him (KI, 126–127/156):

> [My grandmother] was one of the most virtuous of Muslims ... I was once present ... when she was praying in the home of my father,

who was one of the best chanters of the Book of God ... My father felt sympathy for her [in her exertions while praying] and told her, "Mother, if you would only stay seated, you could still say your prayers in that position." She replied, "My dear son, are there days left of my life to enable me to survive to another night like this? No, by God, I shall not sit down." At that time my father was in his seventies, while she was almost a hundred.

And, of course, there was poetry. In his later life and after his death, Usama would be known above all as a poet and it was during these early years at Shayzar that he acquired the necessary skills to discover, engage, and enrich this art. His early tutoring in the Qur'an, grammar, and rhetoric would have given him a sense of the possibilities inherent in the Arabic language. His family, especially his father and his brothers, also composed poems, as befitted noble Arabs of their day. Shayzar, particularly under his uncle Sultan's rule, attracted poets and literati from farther afield who instructed Usama simply by example. In all these sources and more, Usama found inspiration to express his own emotional memory of moments both glorious and mundane, from great victories in battle, to the pain of heartbreak and loneliness, and even to the wiggling of a loose tooth. For most people, these were all very different experiences; but, Usama must have learned, for poets there is much that makes them the same.

EXILE

For Usama, the early thirties were his golden years. He had founded his household, established a family, and, in his son Murhaf, begotten an heir. He had become a skilled hunter and renowned warrior, a courtier who shone from the steady polish of a lifetime of *adab*. Finally, it must have seemed to him, he was a comfort to his father, and beloved by the rest of the Banu Munqidh.

The reality was rather different. Usama was oblivious that his successes had fostered venom among his own kin. One day, he tells us, he went out hunting with his father and a large company, including his uncle Sultan's sons. They came across a particularly fierce lion that had taken refuge on a nearby hillside that could not be approached without dire consequences. Eventually, Usama devised a stratagem by which he rode to the top of the hill above the lion and killed it. The party returned to Shayzar, carrying the lion; Usama was exultant. By the time of their arrival, evening had come. Usama continues (KI, 125–127/154–156):

> As we entered, my paternal grandmother met me in the dark, holding in front of her a lighted candle ... I entertained no doubt that she had come to congratulate me on my safety and acquaint me with her great satisfaction at what I had done. So I met her and kissed her hand. But she said to me with anger and irritation, "My boy, what makes you face these adventures ... and increase the antipathy and ill-will that your uncle carries in his heart against you?" I replied, "Grandmother, the only thing that makes me expose myself to danger ... is to endear myself to the heart of my uncle." She said, "No, by God! On the contrary, this only alienates you from him [because of envy] and makes him feel more antipathy and ill-will toward you."

In later life, Usama would see this as an example of the nobility and sagacity of old women. At the time, however, the warning seems not to have registered with the self-assured young man. For later, news came to Shayzar that a rogue lion was attacking passers-by in the vicinity. Sultan arranged for a great hunting party to be ready the next morning to track the beast down and kill it. Usama, however, could not wait to prove himself again. He slipped out with a page, cornered the lion, and killed it. He returned to Shayzar in triumph, with the lion's head as a trophy. That night, his uncle woke him and asked him to accompany him for what people today politely call "a little chat" (Ibn al-'Adim, *Bughya*, 1988, 3:1363–1364):

> I rode with him until I was quite far from Shayzar, then he said to me: "Nephew, Shayzar is yours, but give it to me! For by God, I can no longer house you here. Sleep would not come to me tonight because of the fury of my thoughts over you, considering what you did with that lion, for what now is to prevent you, should you set your mind to it, from murdering me? Neither sleep nor repose came to me until I decided to expel you, for I cannot house you here while you are capable of such things."

Of course, this is Usama's version. Given that he would spend the rest of his life exiled from Shayzar and forever wishing to regain it, it suited him to explain his expulsion as due purely to his uncle's jealousy of his prowess. In fact, the overweening sons of Murshid were a source of great consternation to their uncle Sultan, and Usama appears to have been the worst of the lot. And Sultan had other anxieties. For, though he might have Shayzar, he was not blessed with progeny as was his older pious brother. Sultan's sons had come later, and none of them, we are told, could match the sons of Murshid in their bravery and refined character.

One can imagine just how obnoxious the precious sons of Murshid would seem to the authoritarian Sultan. While he grew anxious about the future of his patrimony should he be killed in battle, Murshid's sons, all perfect little gentlemen, were excelling even their father in courtliness and feats of bravery and cunning. When Sultan eventually did become a father of sons, he was able, for a time, to reconcile himself to his nephews. But Usama's arrogance must have rankled. Murshid had refused the primacy of Shayzar, and as he settled in to old age, Sultan was effectively its sole lord. Why might the castle and all its lands not be passed down to his children? The continued presence of Murshid's sons, above all the noxious Usama, prevented a ready answer to that question. As close kin, Usama could not honorably be murdered, like an enemy. But he, and eventually all his brothers, could be induced to leave Shayzar and the sons of Sultan for good. Usama finally took the hint. He departed on June 6, 1131 and sought service elsewhere.

SERVICE TO ZANGI

Usama found service almost immediately, or rather, it found him. The precise sequence of events is quite vague; Usama breezes over them, but a manuscript of his anthology of poetry tells us that he headed for Homs, where he was involved in a battle with the man who would become his next patron: Zangi, atabeg of Mosul ('Abbas, Usama, 1981, 83–84).

Zangi of Mosul bore the title of atabeg, indicating his honored status in the Saljuq court as tutor of a prince and *de facto* governor. What the title did not convey was that he was a ruthless and ambitious ruler, who gladly proclaimed holy war against the Franks, while at the same time attacking and neutralizing any Muslim lord that stood in his way. In June 1128, he had added the principality of Aleppo to his Iraqi lands, and set his sights on the Syrian lords to the south. On September 3, 1131, some months after Usama had left Shayzar, Zangi captured the nearby city of Hama. By this time Usama had made his way to the adjacent city of Homs, where he presumably worked in the employ of that city's lord, Kir-Khan ibn Qaraja. When Zangi captured Hama, Kir-Khan of Homs offered to purchase the city from him. Zangi agreed to the deal, but, betraying Kir-Khan at the last minute, attacked his troops and captured Homs for himself. Kir-Khan was taken prisoner, tortured, and carried off to Mosul (Ibn al-'Adim, *Zubda*, 1968, 2:246).

In this battle, Usama was taken captive by Zangi's forces and imprisoned in Hama. He was released shortly after and entered the service of the atabeg. From what little evidence exists, it appears he worked primarily as an amir under Zangi's major-domo, the brutish al-Yaghisiyani, who was eventually made lord of Hama. That is, when Usama mentions his actions during this period in his "memoirs," he is usually based in Hama or in the company of al-Yaghisiyani.

For a relatively sheltered commander like Usama, service under Zangi provided a quick way to become battle-hardened and independent. He certainly appears to have landed on his feet, for, at various places in northern Iraq, he took the opportunity to accompany Zangi on the hunt (KI, 192–193/222–224). In November 1131, he was in Zangi's capital, Mosul, hosting fellow poets. But it was primarily as a warrior that he proved of worth to Zangi. The atabeg was ever on the move, either conquering new lands in Syria, or securing old ones in northern Iraq and beyond. In 1132, Zangi became actively involved in a dispute between four claimants to the Saljuq throne, and Usama found himself fighting alongside him against the armies of the Abbasid caliph himself, at Baghdad. Zangi's troops failed, and he was forced to retreat to Mosul. His foes almost intercepted him at the river town of Tikrit, but the governor there, Ayyub, did him a favor and arranged for Zangi and his men to cross safely. This Ayyub would soon become the father of a boy, Yusuf, who eventually took the title of Salah al-Din (Saladin). And this Saladin would grow up to become the most famous counter-crusader of his time, founder of the Ayyubid dynasty, and, little did he know, Usama's last patron.

In 1134, Zangi (and Usama) spent months on campaign in northern Iraq and Armenia, to no great success. When, in late 1134, Zangi received an invitation from the beleaguered lord of Damascus to take the city, Usama accompanied him. In early 1135, Usama therefore returned to Syria for the first time since his exile. He and his commander al-Yaghisiyani encountered a large contingent of the cavalry of Damascus north of the city, and they would almost certainly have been captured had they not been able, by a ruse, to convince the Damascenes that they faced a much larger force. Happily, Zangi arrived with a real army in the nick of time, though he dressed al-Yaghisiyani down for his audacity. After a long stand-off, Zangi was obliged to withdraw to Mosul and leave Damascus uncaptured. On the way back, he named al-Yaghisiyani governor of Hama. Usama assisted in some of Zangi's later campaigns against Frankish positions in northern Syria and later at Rafaniya near Hama. But, for the most part, Usama and his commander al-Yaghisiyani remained based in Hama, just a day's ride from Shayzar. One wonders what Usama must have thought when he learned that Shayzar, too, had surrendered to the might of the atabeg.

LAST DAYS IN HAMA

Al-Yaghisiyani was a violent and impulsive commander. Service under such a grim figure must have been trying and Usama's recollections stress his brutality. Al-Yaghisiyani had once cut an overly insistent attendant in two, and he took Christians and Jews captive, even though this violated Islamic law. Zangi used to say that al-Yaghisiyani feared neither Zangi nor God Himself, so great were his excesses (KI, 156–157/187–189). Still, Usama proved himself to his commander many times in battle and impressed him greatly with his constant readiness (KI, 99/129–130).

Although he had been expelled from Shayzar and was in service in Hama, Usama appears not to have completely severed all ties with his kin. For example, his own family and household, including his young son Murhaf, appear to have remained there. In the end, it was only the direst of events that drove Usama to return when black news reached him: his father, Murshid, was dying. Thanks to Usama's writings, his father has come down to us almost frozen in time, as a perennially grizzled warrior and hunter but, in his later years, Murshid was greatly enfeebled. On May 30, 1137, at the age of sixty-nine, he died a quiet death in his own bed, and was buried in his house at Shayzar. As he lay dying, he asked his sons to bury him alongside his most treasured possessions: forty-three copies of the Qur'an that he had himself transcribed in his own beautiful calligraphy. Usama returned to Hama after his father's death, but one final report of bad news was to come before he would again be on the move.

In the spring of 1138, Usama learned that the Byzantine emperor John Comnenus had, with help from his Frankish allies, advanced into northern Syria. By April, the Byzantines were putting Shayzar, and Usama's clan, under siege. The closest figure of authority in the region, al-Yaghisiyani, wavered about how to meet this foe, and considered asking Zangi in Mosul to come to his assistance. But Usama saw his moment, and begged al-Yaghisiyani to let him gather supplies, return home, and thereby secure Shayzar for him. Whether, in this plan, Usama saw himself or his uncle Sultan as lord of Shayzar remains an open question. Al-Yaghisiyani agreed, but apparently changed his mind for, the next day, he summoned Usama and ordered him to prepare to march with him to Mosul. Usama was nonplussed. "Shall I leave my children, my brothers, and my womenfolk under siege and proceed to Mosul?", he asked himself. He assented to his commander's orders, but requested to return to Shayzar to collect his family and other supplies for the journey. When he reached the castle, his heart sank. He had come too late (KI, 3/27):

> The enemy had defeated my son and fought their way as far as my home, from which they carried away all the tents, weapons, and furniture that were there, captured my beloved ones and put to flight my comrades. The calamity was great and terrible.

The Banu Munqidh had fought bravely against their besiegers, but the sheer number of Byzantine and Frankish troops overwhelmed them. The lower town had been the scene of panic as the people fled to the citadel for safety, fearing the imminent entrance of Byzantine troops. But the citadel itself had then been subjected to a merciless pounding from Byzantine mangonels. With the countryside pillaged, casualties mounting, and the very walls of his town and family home crumbling, Sultan had sent messengers to the emperor and proposed a truce. In return for a large amount of money and treasure, and fearful of reports of a Muslim relief army, the emperor and his allies had been induced to lift the siege and withdraw, a process completed by May 21, 1138. In response to Sultan's call for aid, Zangi arrived just in time to harass the retreating enemy troops.

In the wake of this major siege, the Banu Munqidh faced the task of repairing the citadel and ransoming captives. But, despite the damage, they could collectively draw a deep breath of relief. The Byzantines had withdrawn and the Franks would no longer pose any extraordinary threat. Shayzar remained in the hands of the Banu Munqidh for years to come. In the late Syrian spring of 1138, as the citadel underwent repair, the wildflowers were in bloom and the falcon hatchlings were yet untried and new to the world. But Usama, an exile returned too late, had little reason to rejoice for long. He collected his son, family and what property he could and left Shayzar and its joys. He would never return.

2

THE OUTCAST AND THE KINGS

Putting the walls of Shayzar behind him, Usama had a number of options. He was, by the time of his exile, a mature man of forty-three, his hair already turning grey, as he would mourn in a poem from this period; the prominent son of a prominent amir from a respected family, known for their courage and social graces. He had defended Shayzar and its domains from attack on numerous occasions. A man in his position might have sought advancement by taking service with one of the regional powers; either the Fatimids in Cairo, or the Saljuq sultan – or even the Abbasid caliph in Baghdad. But these were distant arenas, and Usama probably still harbored hopes of reconciliation with his uncle Sultan, if not outright control of Shayzar. The simplest choice would have been to continue in the service of the atabeg Zangi, whom he had served capably. However, contrary to all expectations, Usama did not return to Zangi, but went to Zangi's rivals in Damascus.

His reasons for moving on remain mysterious, for he simply glosses over his decision and information on his movements in the months after he left Shayzar is vague. When the Byzantines laid siege to Shayzar, Usama had left his post to go to his family's aid, promising his commander that after the battle he would return to Hama and thence to Mosul. But the precise sequence of events once he left Shayzar is not at all clear. Whether he broke with Zangi in Mosul, in Hama, or in some other location altogether is unknown.

Some sense can be made of Usama's decision. What he required was a court in which he could serve to his benefit, but which was located close enough to Shayzar that he could seize any opportunities to return that came his way. Whatever his reasoning, he and his family, including his young son Murhaf, and eventually his brothers and their families, all made their way to Damascus. He was to spend the next few years there, during which time he was to have some of his most memorable experiences with his Frankish neighbors.

DAMASCUS (1138–1144)

When Usama arrived, Damascus was governed by princes of a Turkish dynasty, the Burids. Although Prince Mahmud nominally ruled the region, real power was firmly in the hands of his powerful vizier, Mu'in al-Din Unur. For Unur, Usama had much to offer. Not only was he an accomplished warrior and courtier, but he had something Unur desperately needed: intimate knowledge of the capabilities and habits of the atabeg Zangi. Zangi may well have been aware of the edge Usama gave Unur, for Usama tells us that Zangi repeatedly demanded he return to his service. But he refused, and Zangi continued his assaults. Zangi's ambitions at this time were clear. He would stop at nothing less than the unification of the old Muslim principalities of Mosul, Aleppo, and Damascus. Mosul and Aleppo were firmly in his control, and only the princes of Damascus, under the tutelage of Unur, stood in the way. For much of Usama's stay in Damascus, Zangi's increasingly bold attempts on the city were a backdrop to his relations with his patron Unur.

The Burids were already at war with another regional power, the Franks of the Latin Kingdom of Jerusalem, and they could not be expected to wage another. In order to concentrate his efforts on the threat presented by Zangi, Unur had to find some way to neutralize that presented by the Latin Kingdom. Who better to sound out the Franks about an alliance than the dashing and courtly Usama, a man already experienced in their ways? Unur may well have taken on Usama for this very purpose, for almost as soon as he arrived in Damascus, Usama went on pilgrimage to Jerusalem. While in this third holiest city of Islam he visited the Haram al-Sharif, and was

conducted to other Muslim holy sites by one of the city's inhabitants (KA, 234–235/115–116). He also made the acquaintance of
members of the Knights Templar, a Crusader military order, some
of whom he would later name as "my friends." But if his mission to
Jerusalem were concerned with diplomacy, it was only conceived
as a preliminary visit, for he soon returned to Damascus, and a full
treaty was concluded later. He spent the next year worrying with
Unur over Zangi's intentions, and passing the time on the hunt. In
1139, when Mahmud, the nominal prince and ruler of Damascus,
fell victim to the daggers of unknown assassins, Unur chose his successor. Unur saw to it that the new prince would be equally pliable as
the old, arranging for Mahmud's brother, Jamal al-Din Muhammad,
former lord of Baalbek, to succeed. Usama remained attached to
Unur: as long as the latter's power grew, so did his.

Perhaps out of gratitude, the new prince Muhammad ceded lands
in Baalbek to Unur, but it took some time for them to change hands
– just long enough for Zangi to make his move. With this important strong point temporarily between masters, Zangi encamped
at Baalbek just as the prince Muhammad left for Damascus. Word
soon reached Unur in Damascus that Zangi's army was small and
that he would need reinforcements to take Baalbek. But there was
a worrying detail: Zangi had sent a messenger to persuade an amir,
Ridwan, to join him. Ridwan was an ousted Fatimid official, and
had a reputation, not unlike Usama's, as a courageous fighter and
man of letters. More importantly for Zangi, "the troops felt special
inclination toward him on account of his generosity" (KI, 17/55).
Unur didn't like the odds should Ridwan decide to join Zangi, and
so he sent Usama to Ridwan, at the fortress of Salkhad in the Hawran
region of central Syria, to try to persuade him to abandon Zangi and
join with them instead.

Arriving in Ridwan's presence, Usama was met with an immov-
able argument: Ridwan had already given his word to join Zangi at
Baalbek, so there was nothing more to be said. But Usama knew that
Ridwan's own sense of self-preservation – he was a refugee from
a failed plot against him in Egypt – would overcome his sense of
honor. Usama confessed that he did not doubt that Zangi sincerely

wanted Ridwan. But to what end? He offered Ridwan a stern warning, as someone who could claim to know Zangi's ways: join him
now, and you will find yourself later paraded before the Saljuq sultan
as a prisoner. "When you have crossed the Euphrates," he slyly suggested, "he will send you before him and boast over the sultans of
the East, saying, 'Behold! This is the ruler of Egypt, who is now in
my service!'" Ridwan thus found his promise to Zangi to be flexible
and arranged to depart for Damascus. In return, he and his companions were to receive cash stipends and lands from Unur. Usama
returned to Damascus to make arrangements for Ridwan's arrival
while Ridwan assembled his men and belongings (KI, 30–31/57).

Usama had made a coup. He had successfully convinced Zangi's
potentially crucial ally not only to renege on his promise, but even
to join forces with Damascus. But, in the end, it all came to naught.
While Usama was in Damascus, a messenger arrived from Egypt,
urging Ridwan and his men to return to Cairo. He couldn't resist
the summons, and so, his travel preparations already underway, he
headed south for Egypt. *En route*, his men mutinied and he only
narrowly escaped death but as we shall see, a more gruesome fate
awaited him. As for Zangi, he seems not to have needed Ridwan's
help: Baalbek fell to the atabeg on October 10, 1139. Usama, Unur,
and the people of Damascus prepared for the worst.

USAMA AMONG THE FRANKS

Happily for Unur and the Damascenes, by early 1140 Usama had successfully negotiated a truce between the Frankish king Fulk of Anjou
and the lord of Damascus. Apparently, Unur was right to choose
Usama; for he credited his success to the fact that King Fulk's wife,
Queen Melisende, was the daughter of Baldwin II, who was indebted
to Usama's father due to the many kindnesses he received while a hostage at Shayzar (KI, 50/110). In the end, Zangi was obliged to withdraw to Mosul, his designs on the principality temporarily frustrated.
The death of the prince Muhammad on March 29, 1140 appears not
to have interrupted the arrangement, and Unur still held sway.

In sequel to the truce of 1140, Usama and Unur traveled at least once, and probably more, to the Kingdom of Jerusalem. At different times between 1140 and 1143, Usama visited Jerusalem, Acre, Nablus, Sebaste, Haifa, and Tiberias, to name only those towns he explicitly recorded, and met and treated with various Frankish leaders and their subjects. These voyages form the context of many of his famous "appreciations of the Frankish character," as Hitti entitled this section of the *Book of Learning by Example*. Usama was rather underwhelmed by what he experienced of Frankish "culture," though he grudgingly gave the Franks credit for their bravery and commitment (see chapter 5).

At Acre, Usama ransomed Muslim prisoners of war, either keeping them as servants for his own home or the Damascus court, or releasing them on the spot (KI, 50–51/110–112). He also noted the trade in exotic animals at the port and, when Unur expressed his pleasure in a certain hunting dog and falcon belonging to a Genoese merchant, King Fulk arranged for them to be sent to Unur straight away (KI, 115–116/226). While passing through Haifa, Usama was again drawn to the animal market, where a Frankish merchant tried to sell him a hunting cheetah, not realizing that it was actually a leopard, which Usama considered a far more dangerous animal (KI, 68/141).

Such interactions could lead to relationships that were more than purely formal. One knight was so taken with Usama that he referred to him as his "brother," and asked him if he might take his son Murhaf back to Europe with him to learn the ways of knighthood. Usama politely demurred, blaming the boy's grandmother's devotion. In fact, he was horrified at the idea, noting that if his son had been taken prisoner, he would at least be able to ransom him straight away (KI, 80/161). Nevertheless, Usama named other Franks as his friends, and noted that those who had been in the region long enough became perfectly decent people (KI, 82/163, 85/169). The zealous new arrivals were the difficult ones, such as the knight who, upon observing Usama praying in the al-Aqsa Mosque in Jerusalem, brusquely turned him to face east, saying, "*This* is the way you should pray!" The Templar knights in the vicinity were horrified at this breach of manners to an honored guest, and apologized to Usama profusely (KI, 82/163–164).

At Sebaste, near Nablus, Usama visited the tomb of John the Baptist, a holy site for both Muslims and Christians. While there, he was deeply impressed by a group of elderly Christian men, bent upon crutches, engaging in their devotions. Indeed, the sight of such exertions and devotion troubled him and made him fear for the future of Islam, until he later witnessed similar zeal on the part of some Muslim mystics – Sufis – in Damascus (KA, 326–327/119).

TROUBLE IN DAMASCUS

With the Latin Kingdom under truce, and Zangi withdrawn to Mosul, there was little fighting left to do in Damascus. Usama diverted himself at the hunt and chasing down bandits, who had become a serious nuisance in the immediate outskirts of the city (KI, 92–93/182–183). But the quiet that had fallen on the world outside the walls of Damascus gave room for commotion within. By 1144, Unur – and Usama with him – was forced to contend with a new rival: not a foreign invader, but a man from within the ranks of the Damascene populace, Ibn al-Sufi, who held the office of urban leader (ra'is). Thanks to their popularity among the people of Damascus, Ibn al-Sufi's family would be an important political power in the city for decades to come. And, while the family had been influential in years past in Aleppo and Damascus, it was really during Usama's stay that they made their name as a force to be reckoned with.

The details of Ibn al-Sufi's activities are far from clear, but local resentment of Turkish rule may have played a part. He was certainly planning a revolt of some kind against Unur, perhaps in order to usurp his position as éminence grise of the new, and rather feckless, prince Abaq. He used his position as urban leader and mouthpiece for the populace to agitate the residents against Unur, who, as a Turk, was seen as an outsider. As Ibn al-Sufi's threats grew more pointed, Unur took to brooding. Rather than relying on the counsel of his companion and right-hand man Usama, whose Syrian connections were obvious, Unur found a new favorite, a fellow Turk, Tuman, another refugee from the court of Zangi.

Usama is, as usual, reticent about just what happened. But it seems clear that Unur and others believed him to be involved in some kind of plot. Unur certainly thought that if Usama was planning something, he was not alone. News reached him of a plot – "ugly things," as the Arabic sources usually describe such unpleasantness – hatched by his vizier, and when the vizier was forced out of his post and fled to the fortress town of Salkhad, Usama was forced out with him. These events become even more puzzling as it was not Unur who eventually went to Salkhad to negotiate with Usama and the vizier, but Unur's rival, Ibn al-Sufi (Ibn al-Qalanisi, *Ta'rikh*, 1983, 434). Something (whatever it was) was afoot in the court of Damascus, and Usama, to judge by a poem he wrote to Unur in his defense, tried in vain to win his trust. Rather than wait around for his innocence to be proven and risk his lord's increasing anxiety, Usama, with his family, belongings, and companion in exile, fled to Egypt, taking only what they could safely carry (KI, 2/28).

EGYPTIAN ADVENTURES (1144–1154)

For a man of Usama's distinction, Egypt was the next logical place to seek his fortune. Then, as ever, a center of civilization, Egypt was the heart of the Fatimid dynasty, and their Nile-side capital, Cairo, was one of the chief cities of the Islamic world, offering limitless opportunities to talented and ambitious people like Usama, on a level rather beyond those in more provincial Damascus. Moreover, Cairo was already home to friends and family. With contacts and resources like these at his disposal, Cairo would be an easy nut to crack.

Usama arrived in Cairo on November 30, 1144 and almost immediately entered the service of the Fatimid caliph, al-Hafiz. He had picked a good time. The city had settled down under the self-appointed al-Hafiz, after nearly a decade of factionalism and *coups d'état*. The caliph's ambitious commanders and viziers and his trouble-some sons had split the regime and exhausted the Fatimid army, and, with a relative peace now restored, he was in need of seasoned men like Usama. But, lurking in Hafiz's Cairo was an ever-present shadow of unrest, one that could reward or crush ambitious politicians.

Whether Usama was fully aware of the currents stirring in his new home or not, he seems to have fit himself into the environment quite well. Having left his family and possessions behind in Ascalon in Palestine while he scouted ahead, he now arranged to have them transported to Cairo although his brother, 'Izz al-Dawla 'Ali, remained behind in Ascalon, to continue the fight against the Franks. Usama was assigned lavish lodgings near the caliphal palace in a mansion that had once belonged to a powerful vizier, and was granted lands northwest of Cairo at Kum Ashfin, in the Delta. The revenues from Kum Ashfin, combined with the wealth he was granted for entering the caliph's service, were more than enough to set him up in style. As in Mosul and Damascus, he enjoyed an urbane social life. Within a few months he was holding poetry salons in his home and hunting waterfowl in the marshes of the Delta like a pharaoh (KI, 2/30, 114–115/224–226).

Having settled into his new life, one wonders what he made of the news coming from his old haunts in Syria. His first patron, the atabeg Zangi, was killed – assassinated – on September 14, 1146. His considerable lands, acquired over a lifetime of conquest, were divided between his two sons; his son Nur al-Din receiving control over Usama's homeland, Syria. In Damascus, Usama's old patron Unur still worked to prevent outright Zangid occupation of his city, even agreeing to recognize Nur al-Din as his formal overlord. Usama never lost touch with Unur and the two remained companions. In 1147, for example, Usama sent Unur a poem congratulating him on his conquest of the contested castle of Salkhad. But Unur did not survive long after repulsing the Franks during the failed Second Crusade against Damascus, for he died on August 30, 1149.

THE LESSON OF RIDWAN

During his stay in Egypt, Usama tried to stay out of trouble and above the political cross-currents in the Fatimid palace. Although he succeeded at first, in the end he failed, and failed miserably. He may well have been inspired by what he saw of the political possibilities in Cairo during the attempted *coup* by Ridwan ibn al-Walakhshi, though he would later use his memory of the same events as a lesson to avoid politics.

This was the same Ridwan that Usama had, years ago, convinced to renege on his promises to assist Zangi during his siege of Baalbek. Ridwan was, by all accounts, an intriguer of the first order. He had been Fatimid vizier earlier in al-Hafiz's reign, but the caliph grew wary of him and encouraged his troops to rebel. This rebellion forced him to flee to Salkhad in Syria, where Usama first encountered him. As we have seen, Ridwan was persuaded to return to Egypt rather than assist Usama and Unur, apparently in the hope of gaining enough loyal troops to stage a *coup* of his own. But as soon as he entered Egypt, his troops rebelled and he was thrown into prison despite al-Hafiz's promise of safe conduct.

When Usama arrived in Cairo in late 1144, Ridwan was still a guest in al-Hafiz's dungeons. However, using an iron nail, and with help from associates on the outside, Ridwan was able to dig his way out and cross the Nile to pyramid-shaded Giza, where troops had rallied to his cause. The city was abuzz with the news of his daring escape. Al-Hafiz readied his troops and sent them against Ridwan's forces, but Ridwan won the day and marched into Cairo in triumph, making the al-Aqmar Mosque, in the north of the city, his headquarters. Usama, who should have been among al-Hafiz's defenders, rode with his men to the palace, but, finding the caliphal doors locked, promptly returned to the safety of his home.

At the al-Aqmar Mosque, supplies and supporters for Ridwan poured in. But, according to Usama, al-Hafiz unleashed a contingent of drunken Sudanese troops who so frightened Ridwan's forces that they fled *en masse*. Ridwan, virtually deserted, was attacked by one of his own men. The Sudanese troops then arrived and killed him on the spot. His body, Usama adds as a comment on the barbarity of the Sudanese troops, was cut into pieces and eaten so that the troops might acquire his bravery (KI, 17–19/55–59).

A NEW PATRON

Usama's account of Ridwan's revolt gives the distinct impression that his attempt at coming to al-Hafiz's aid was half-hearted, and he may well have sensed which way the political winds were blowing. With his old friend and protector Unur dead, and the aging al-Hafiz's health failing, Usama probably keenly felt the need to locate a future patron and protector. Ridwan too was dead, but other candidates would come to the fore. Usama seems to have decided to take steps to ensure his access to a stable source of patronage, involving himself in the course of Egyptian politics to a degree to which he never before dared.

In the autumn of 1149, Cairo was stirring with political possibilities. Ten years had passed with a weakling on the throne and the post of vizier empty. Civil war gripped Fatimid Egypt, as different factions vied for power. In September, a contingent of the caliphal guard was wiped out. Ordinary citizens locked themselves in their houses as the troops ran amok. Usama and his men remained armed and barricaded day and night. Al-Hafiz was too infirm to punish the mutineers, and died less than a month later, on October 10, 1149 to be succeeded by his seventeen-year-old son al-Zafir.

Al-Zafir started out energetically. He gained the allegiance of the troops and, following his father's instructions, filled the all-important vacant post of vizier with an aging amir of his father's regime, Ibn Masal. But this news came as a distinct slap in the face to another amir, Ibn al-Sallar, who had served his father well as governor of Alexandria and had hoped he would be named vizier. He decided to make an issue of it, and, unfortunately for al-Zafir, had friends in Cairo to assist him. Almost immediately after pledging their allegiance to Ibn Masal, most of the troops of Egypt were persuaded to abandon him and support Ibn al-Sallar. For his part, al-Zafir gathered what troops he could and, setting Ibn Masal at their head, sent them out to collect more from the Arab and Berber tribes of the Delta.

While Ibn Masal was in the Delta, his rival Ibn al-Sallar managed to slip into Cairo and occupy the vizier's palace unopposed. He then secured the allegiance of the army, including Usama. He assigned

Usama and his household a house, ordering them to remain inside for the time being. He then sent his son, the amir al-'Abbas, at the head of a contingent of troops, to intercept Ibn Masal upon his return. Unhappily, things went badly. Al-'Abbas's troops began to desert him and Ibn Masal's Bedouin contingents harassed his camp day and night. Ibn al-Sallar sought the counsel of Usama, who agreed to ride out with him to al-'Abbas's rescue the following morning. Ibn Masal's forces were routed and most were slaughtered. Al-'Abbas killed Ibn Masal with his own hands. Nothing was left to impede Ibn al-Sallar's rise, and he, al-'Abbas, and Usama returned victorious to Cairo.

Al-Zafir was obliged to recognize Ibn al-Sallar as his new vizier, but not without bitterness. Indeed, by the end of January 1150, al-Zafir had arranged to have him assassinated while he slept. But Ibn al-Sallar was informed of the plot by one of his servants and the assassins were chased down and all who were captured killed. With that particular menace foiled, Ibn al-Sallar could turn to the business of appeasing the troops that had so warmly supported him, offering the prospect of glory and the spoils of war against the Franks. Baldwin III, the king of Jerusalem, had already begun his plans to re-fortify the city of Gaza, from which he hoped to take the Fatimid bastion of Ascalon. To distract the Franks, and thereby allow the Fatimids to launch an assault from Ascalon, Ibn al-Sallar wished to enlist the support of Nur al-Din in Syria and encourage him to attack the Frankish city of Tiberias. With Frankish energies focused on Nur al-Din's attack in the north, Ascalon and the south would be open to Fatimid attacks.

AN EXPEDITION TO SYRIA

To assist him in persuading Nur al-Din, Ibn al-Sallar enlisted the talents of Usama, who was to ride to Syria with a cargo of treasure and a group of Arab guides. If Nur al-Din rejected the plan, then Usama was to enlist what troops he could and march back to Ascalon, to await further orders. Usama entered Syria by way of Sinai, ever on the lookout for Frankish soldiers. But he and his company, although they did encounter a pariah tribe of Arabs, met no Franks, nearly lost most of the treasure, and only narrowly avoided losing their way altogether. In the end, in about May 1150, Usama arrived at the ancient Syrian city of Bosra, where the old Roman amphitheatre had been converted into a fortress. At Bosra, Usama learned that Nur al-Din was encamped before the walls of Damascus, in the hope of realizing the conquest his father Zangi had never been able to achieve. Shortly after Usama came to Bosra, Nur al-Din's general Shirkuh arrived, and he and Usama returned to the armies at Damascus, where Usama gained his interview with Nur al-Din.

Usama's first encounter with Nur al-Din was important for his future career, for it created a connection to a ruler whose star at that very moment was in the ascendant. This connection would prove invaluable. For Ibn al-Sallar, the interview was less of a boon. Usama presented his arguments, but Nur al-Din replied that he was effectively worse off than the Fatimids, caught as he was between Franks to the south and enemies in Damascus to the north. In the end, Nur al-Din could offer only nominal support: a contingent of thirty horsemen led by none other than Tuman al-Yaruqi, Usama's old rival from Unur's court. Usama was thus forced into his alternative mission. He raised what troops he could from those men whom Nur al-Din had rejected from his Damascus campaign, and marched in stages toward Ascalon, by-passing the frontiers of the Latin Kingdom.

Toward the end of 1150, Usama and his troops arrived at Ascalon, where Usama sought out his brother 'Ali, who, with his own followers, had been fighting the Franks for the past few years. For about four months, the two brothers battled against a common enemy. Indeed, no sooner had Usama and his men arrived in the city than a Frankish army attacked, to be repulsed by Usama's men. He was also involved in Muslim campaigns against Frankish castles, as at Bayt Jibrin, where the over-cautious Franks allowed his troops to slip by unopposed, or as at Yubna (Frankish Ibelin), where a small number of Frankish prisoners were taken. But he eventually received a summons from the vizier Ibn al-Sallar urging him to return to Cairo, and so he was never able to participate in Ascalon's larger campaign against Frankish-held Gaza. During that campaign, in 1151 or early 1152, his brother 'Ali was killed, a heavy blow to Usama, who, at fifty-five, was himself approaching what for his time was old age. 'Ali, Usama said in reporting his brother's death, "was one of the most distinguished savants, cavaliers, and devout men among the Muslims," a martyr "who fought for the sake of religion and not for the sake of this world" (KI, 3–9/31–42).

CONSPIRACY IN CAIRO

Usama returned to Cairo, and reintegrated himself into the life of the Fatimid court, with all the intrigues that implies. The caliph, al-Zafir, still resented the presence of the vizier Ibn al-Sallar, who had foiled one attempt on his life already, and was never his own choice to begin with. Moreover, although Ibn al-Sallar was Usama's patron and badly needed him for an upcoming campaign, Usama was spending more and more time in the service of Ibn al-Sallar's ambitious stepson, the amir al-'Abbas. The subtly shifting loyalties surrounding Ibn al-Sallar eventually coalesced and brought about his death. Usama, an eyewitness, explained the events thus: al-'Abbas had a young son, Nasr, about the same age as the caliph al-Zafir. The caliph and Nasr were close companions and became lovers. In the spring of 1153, Ibn al-Sallar launched yet another campaign to defend Ascalon. Among the leaders of the armies were Usama and al-'Abbas, who brought with him his son Nasr. However, just a few days march from Cairo, near the Delta town of Bilbays, Nasr took leave of his father and, without permission, abandoned the troops and returned to Cairo, presumably because army life bored him.

Al-Zafir and Nasr had secretly worked out a plan whereby Nasr, being a member of Ibn al-Sallar's extended household, would enable a small group of al-Zafir's guard to make their way into Ibn al-Sallar's house and murder him while he slept. The plot was accomplished, and Ibn al-Sallar was killed on April 3, 1153. When news of his death reached his men, they rushed out and assaulted the caliphal palace. Eventually, the troops accepted the fact of the matter and

surrendered, offering their loyalties either to the amir Nasr or his
father al-'Abbas, who became Ibn al-Sallar's replacement as all-
powerful vizier (KI, 18–19/42–44).

One need not be a great detective to see that, in becoming the
new vizier, only al-'Abbas really benefited from the murder of Ibn
al-Sallar. Of course, as son of the new vizier, Nasr would benefit
indirectly. But that was also the case for Usama, who was now in
service to al-'Abbas. Clearly, there is something more behind these
happenings: other chronicles have a rather different version of the
events surrounding Ibn al-Sallar's death, and do not reflect favorably
on Usama's role. According to these accounts, matters turned sour
on the march from Cairo. While camped in the Delta, Usama and
al-'Abbas got to talking about the hardships of combat and compared
them to the luxury and ease of life in Cairo. Al-'Abbas yearned to
return, and cursed Ibn al-Sallar for commanding such a dreary campaign. At this, Usama slyly suggested to al-'Abbas that, if he wanted
to, he could become ruler of Egypt. And so the plot was hatched:
al-'Abbas was to encourage his son Nasr in enlisting the support of
his lover al-Zafir to assassinate Ibn al-Sallar and name al-'Abbas in
his place. Usama and al-'Abbas conferred with Nasr and sent him
on his way to Cairo to the murder of Ibn al-Sallar (e.g., Ibn al-Athir,
al-Kamil, 1966, 11:191).

Writing of these events in his *Book of Learning by Example*, Usama
was telling only half of the story, and tidied it up, depicting himself
observing from the sidelines, when it seems more likely that he was
in fact their instigator. Even if Usama's account is to be believed, it
does leave open the question of whether he has faithfully depicted his
role in other intrigues that seem to have hounded him, from Shayzar,
to Hama, and to Damascus.

THE FINAL STRAW

Usama's political activities did not end with the accession of al-
'Abbas as vizier. According to Usama, al-'Abbas and his son Nasr
were increasingly at odds. Al-'Abbas suspected that Nasr had other

tricks up his sleeve, and the people were ever more resentful of al-'Abbas's leadership since Ascalon had disastrously fallen to Frankish troops in September 1153. Usama tried to reconcile the two, but to no real end. Nasr could no longer bear his father's reproaches, and at the instigation of the caliph al-Zafir, decided to kill him and to take his place. Usama, it should be mentioned, was seen less and less with al-'Abbas, devoting himself to the service of Nasr, perhaps an indication that the political winds had shifted yet again. Eventually, Nasr sought Usama's counsel on his plan to murder his father, and Usama dissuaded him; political assassination was one thing, but patricide was abhorrent. The next day, Nasr made a clean breast of the whole plot to his father who, though furious, won over his son's allegiance and the two plotted the downfall of their shared obstacle to glory: the bloody-minded caliph al-Zafir, whose absence would benefit everyone. Significantly, the chroniclers have a slightly different version: according to them, it was Usama who instigated the murder of al-Zafir pointing out to al-'Abbas the shame that his son's relationship with the caliph was bringing upon him. Usama's appeal to al-'Abbas's sense of propriety seems to have worked, for the caliph was murdered in the company of Nasr on April 15, 1154 and his body was thrown into a pit in Nasr's house.

The next morning, al-'Abbas feigned surprise over the caliph's absence from his customary morning audience. When it was ascertained that the caliph was nowhere to be found, al-'Abbas named al-Zafir's infant son as his successor, taking the title of al-Fa'iz. He was proclaimed before the people, riding on the shoulders of one of the court eunuchs. As al-Fa'iz was gingerly seated on his oversized throne, al-'Abbas had a body of his troops apprehend the brothers of the murdered al-Zafir and kill them. It was an inglorious moment for Egypt. If Cairo was in tumult before al-'Abbas arrived on the scene, it now exploded into civil war.

Al-'Abbas's brazenness did not endear him either to the people or the troops of Cairo. Al-Zafir's surviving sisters had formed a pretty clear idea of what had happened and wrote to a powerful amir, loyal to their family, who was absent administering his province in Upper Egypt. This was al-Tala'i' ibn Ruzzik, who had become an acquaintance of Usama's. Ibn Ruzzik wasted no time in answering the calls of the princesses for help and set out with a small army for Cairo. That same day, April 26, 1154, al-'Abbas ordered ships to be sent up the Nile against Ibn Ruzzik and troops to march out and confront him. He ordered Nasr and Usama to remain in the city, and marched out at the head of his army.

But his army had other plans. Most of his troops mutinied on the spot, refusing to follow him and locking the gates of Cairo behind them. It was not a brilliant plan, for a battle then ensued during which the rebel troops inside the walls both fought street-to-street against those troops inside the city still loyal to al-'Abbas (notably those of Usama and Nasr) and against al-'Abbas himself outside. Eventually, the rebels fled and al-'Abbas pursued and killed those he could. But if the material goals of the rebellion failed, its message was received. Al-'Abbas resolved that he could no longer trust the army and, thus, could no longer remain in Egypt. Abandoning Egypt to Ibn Ruzzik, he began making plans to flee to Syria, to the succor of Nur al-Din (KI, 23–24/48–50).

Al-'Abbas, well aware of Usama's friendship with Ibn Ruzzik, made him swear solemn oaths that he would not desert and would come to Syria with him. Usama had a difficult choice. With his companion Ibn Ruzzik as vizier and a child as caliph, his position in Egypt would effectively be the same as if al-'Abbas had remained. Better, in fact, because the troops genuinely seemed to obey Ibn Ruzzik. On the other hand, flight with al-'Abbas into Syria offered the hope of a return to Shayzar and, who could say, perhaps, with Nur al-Din's help, a return to Egypt? In the end, possibly because his involvement in al-'Abbas's *coup* had so badly damaged his standing in Cairo, he swore his oaths and prepared for the trip to Syria. Ibn Ruzzik begged him to reconsider, but to no avail.

While al-'Abbas fended off an assault by rebellious troops, and his house was given up to general plunder, Usama assembled his and al-'Abbas's families and everyone regrouped outside the northern walls of Cairo. The troops shut the gates behind them and looted the city. Usama lost nearly everything. Moreover, as he and his party progressed through the Delta, Arab tribesmen harassed them day and night for six days. During one encounter, Usama was very nearly killed. When the Arabs had dispersed, on June 6, 1154, Usama realized that his family would never survive such a journey. He therefore sent them back from Bilbays to Cairo where Ibn Ruzzik took care of them and treated them with kindness. Usama remembered taking a moment to reflect on the vicissitudes of Fate (KI, 26/52):

> We all set out with none of us having a handful of provisions. When I wanted to drink, I would dismount and drink from the palm of my hand, while the night before I started, as I was sitting on a chair in one of the hallways of my home, somebody had offered me sixteen camels for carrying water, with as many as God the praiseworthy wanted of water and food bags.

The next morning, in a mountainous region at the borders of Fatimid Egypt and the Latin Kingdom, a contingent of Frankish soldiers caught sight of Usama's retinue and attacked. During the fighting, al-'Abbas was killed and Nasr taken prisoner, along with Usama's brother, Muhammad. Usama assembled what few of the routed men he could and fled to the hills. As for Nasr, some sources suggest he expressed a willingness to convert to Christianity and had even started studying Latin while in captivity. Instead, the Templars ransomed him back to Ibn Ruzzik, who had him executed. His corpse was suspended upon the southern gate of Cairo for no less than two years as a reminder and a warning to all who attempted to meddle in politics.

Usama and his men avoided death at the hands of the Franks, only to find themselves the favorite targets of the nomadic tribes of the area. As they progressed, virtually unarmed and without food or water, into what is now southern Jordan, they were attacked almost without cease by Bedouin. Finally, upon reaching Wadi Musa, the wide and stony valley that leads from the Gulf of 'Aqaba to the ancient stone-carved city of Petra, Usama knew himself to be in the territory of familiar tribes. He asked some Bedouin who the leader of the tribes encamped in the valley might be, and this turned out to be an acquaintance. Usama sent a message to him, and the next day he was received with customary hospitality. Usama and his men were now refreshed and rested and his friend led them out of his territory and toward Damascus, whose encircling green gardens they sighted on June 19, 1154 (KI, 24–28 / 50–54).

DAMASCUS AND NUR AL-DIN (1154–1164)

Only two months earlier, Nur al-Din had finally taken Damascus from the Burid prince Abaq, after the people had opened the gates of the city to him. Ibn al-Sufi, the other remaining political force in the city, died of natural causes one month after Nur al-Din's conquest. The city was thus open to its new ruler's designs. Nur al-Din spent much of his time either in Aleppo or on campaign, so he put his trusted general Shirkuh in command of the province of Damascus. Fortunately for Usama, Shirkuh was an acquaintance from his time with the atabeg Zangi, which facilitated his entry into the service of Nur al-Din. Shirkuh was also the uncle of Saladin, which would be of some importance when Nur al-Din later sent both uncle and nephew to conquer Egypt.

Usama's absence was sorely felt in Egypt. Ibn Ruzzik applied constant pressure for him to return now that the unrest there had settled down. Ibn Ruzzik may well have felt the same way Zangi had years earlier when Usama abandoned him for the court of Unur: fearful. For now a man with intimate knowledge of his powers and habits had entered the service of a potential enemy. Nor could Usama have been comforted by Ibn Ruzzik's demands. After all, his family and most of his belongings were still in his hands; Ibn Ruzzik effectively held them hostage, answering Usama's requests with the reply that he could have them when he returned to Egypt. And, Ibn Ruzzik added by way of sweetening the pot, if Cairo no longer suited him, then he would grant him the southern frontier town of Aswan, from which he could wage war on the Abyssinians to his content. Not wanting to risk Ibn Ruzzik's anger, Usama politely demurred and fended off the vizier's request without raising his ire. Indeed, the two continued a poetic correspondence during Usama's early years in Damascus (e.g. *Diwan*, 111–112, 136, etc.).

The well-being of Usama's household, held hostage in Egypt, troubled him, especially as his mother had died. Eventually, he was able to convince Nur al-Din to arrange for their removal to Damascus. Such a voyage required an oath of safe conduct from the Frankish king of Jerusalem, Baldwin III, which Nur al-Din's considerable persuasion procured. The safe conduct proved to be worthless. *En route* from Damietta to the port of Acre, a group of Frankish sailors, apparently under the command of the king, attacked the boat bearing Usama's family and pillaged its contents. The king claimed it was his legal due by right of salvage, and sent Usama's family on to Damascus with just a few dinars to support them. Usama took the loss of his personal library, the one relatively constant companion in his life, especially hard (KI, 19–20/60–61):

> The safety of my children, my brother's children, and our women made the loss of money which we suffered a comparatively easy matter to endure – with the exception of the books, which were four thousand volumes, all of the most valuable kind. Their loss has left a heartache that will stay with me to the last day of my life.

In the spring of 1156, while Usama's family was being delivered from Acre to Damascus, he himself was far to the north on campaign with Nur al-Din. Nur al-Din had decided to attempt to wrest control of two fortified towns from the lands of his northern neighbor, the Saljuq sultan of Anatolia. By the autumn of 1156, Usama had returned to Damascus to be reunited with his family. It was then that his thoughts turned to his brother Muhammad, who had been captured when they fled Egypt. Usama first tried asking his cousin (also Muhammad), the current lord of Shayzar, for help, but he refused. And so Usama begged Nur al-Din to do what he could, and he and the Frankish king arranged a prisoner exchange: Nur al-Din released a high-ranking Templar, and in return, Usama's brother was sent to Damascus. Save for Shayzar itself, Usama had salvaged everything he possibly could from his wandering days of adventures and misadventures.

In service to a powerful prince, family and household reconstituted in a city he called home, Usama could now consider his relationship to Shayzar at leisure. His uncle Sultan, who had expelled him and his brothers, had recently died. During these months Usama sent a poem to his cousin, Muhammad, Sultan's son and the current lord of Shayzar. His task was manifold: to praise his deceased uncle, father of the poem's recipient, and yet wonder at the source of his ancient anger. Along the way, he must also laud Muhammad as the new lord of Shayzar and hope for amnesty now that Sultan was dead. The poem was a long one, but even an excerpt conveys Usama's plight (*Diwan*, 27):

> Why is it that I see between us and the home, a gathering-place
> A place of closeness to your sympathy, only remoteness and distance?
> Do not hasten toward a separation which will overtake us;
> The vicissitudes of Time suffice us well enough as our lot.
> Rather accept a heart, that, when I have quieted its pangs
> Merely races, and tears, when I hold them back, merely flood.
> You have my love; even if you act unjustly, your injustice
> I consider a bounty from you, as long as it is not overmuch.

Muhammad's reaction is not recorded. And, in the end, it doesn't matter. For on one fateful summer day, Muhammad, Shayzar, the Banu Munqidh, and everything that represented Usama's past life, were virtually wiped off the face of the earth.

CALAMITY

The birds will have felt it first, then everyone else, all at once. In August 1157, a powerful earthquake struck northern Syria, leveling cities and killing thousands. It visited disaster indiscriminately upon Frankish and Muslim territories alike: the Frankish fortresses of Crac des Chevaliers and 'Irqa, the port cities of Latakia, Tripoli, and even mighty Antioch were all badly affected; for the Muslims, the cities of Aleppo, Hama, and Homs, and smaller towns such as Kafartab, Apamea, and Ma'arrat al-Nu'man were struck. But nowhere was the loss felt more greatly than at Shayzar. On that August day, almost every member of the Banu Munqidh, apart from Usama and his household in Damascus, were gathered in one of the main halls of the home of Muhammad ibn Sultan, the current lord of Shayzar, the cousin to whom Usama had sent his poetic request for amnesty. The celebration marked the circumcision of one of Muhammad's sons. As the earthquake struck the citadel fell down upon them, killing all but one. The survivor was the wife of Muhammad ibn Sultan, who was pulled from the rubble still breathing. Another son of Sultan, Isma'il, unable to attend the festivities, also survived the catastrophe. For Usama, it was a disaster from which he would never fully recover.

In time, Usama grew philosophical about the destruction of his home and kin, seeing in it the designs of fortune, as in this fragment lamenting the loss of the scenes of his youth (MD, 303–304):

> Moisture-swollen rain-clouds pour abundantly on their dwelling
> And the dry and withered gardens burst into blossom.
> The delicious nights that had ceased have returned there
> And the ease and sweetness of life that had passed.
> A gift, hoped for though unattainable
> By one who hopes too far, heartsick, lost.
> Dwellings, in which I passed the bloom of my youth
> At times in earnest endeavor, at times in playful frolick.
> Now come I to the pastimes of childhood and its delights
> Now go I before a brave lion, and fall upon him.
> There I knew the antelope's eye glimpsed outside her veil:
> A savage lion, whoever meets it meets death!
> And a herd of gazelles, beside whom the sun is veiled
> And whose old women veil themselves even before the ghosts of the past.
> Each of my brothers was as brave and noble as you can imagine:
> Their swords are drawn freshly polished.
> Nothing of what was remains but misfortune
> And sorrows of the heart, whose bedlam never ceases.
> I used to believe that that which gave me joy was not fleeting
> But he who is ignorant of the path of prudence will lose his way.
> For it is all but a vision reckoned while drowsing
> As real. And that which dissipates sleep, dissipates its falsities.

The dramatic and fateful nature of the destruction of Shayzar and the sudden elimination of so noble a house was not lost on other poets, who saw in it a lesson on the unknowable designs of Fate, comparing it to the swift end of the Barmakid family in early Islamic times, and using it to meditate upon Him whose power and might did not decline. Even Ibn Ruzzik, writing in consolation, urged him never to forget that Fortune obeys its own rules (MD, 79–80):

> My soul grieves for dwellings, of their inhabitants
> Emptied, not a single one remaining.
> A slap, a grave occurrence that disperses them, making him
> Forget the homelands of his youth and his family in one day.
> Take measure of what has befallen your people, Majd al-Din [i.e., Usama]
> And bear up, for the accidents of Fate will keep coming like a flurry
> of blows.
> For such is Fate, its judgments are both unfairness and
> Justice, involving things both hateful and admirable.
> If Misfortune has selected you, then it
> Will continue to visit upon you and nobody else.
> It is like a spear, that on that fateful day,
> Cleaves your heart but leaves you standing on your own two feet.

In the months that followed, various groups tried to take possession of the ruins of Shayzar in the hope of rebuilding it. The Franks attacked in October 1157, to be repulsed by a group of Muslims. But it was Nur al-Din who finally captured the site and began restoring it, giving the ruins to his trusted lieutenant Ibn al-Daya, whose family ruled Shayzar, with some interruptions, for another seventy-five years, ever mindful of the prouder family that once ruled there and the fate that befell them.

In Damascus, Usama continued to reflect on these events, compose poetry, and correspond with friends. His old friend Ibn Ruzzik still pressed him to return to Egypt, but then suddenly changed his requests. In April 1158, Ibn Ruzzik's troops had won a major victory against the Franks at Ascalon. Now was the time for joint action, and he urged Usama to convince Nur al-Din to take to the field with the Egyptians. But Nur al-Din could not be convinced. It may be that, based in Syria as he was, he had a better sense of the political and military realities of such an attack. Nur al-Din was to remain something of a loner in his military pursuits, preferring to concentrate his energies on Frankish targets whose capture benefited him alone.

After a brief scare when rumors circulated that Nur al-Din had suddenly died of an illness, genuine tidings of death came from Egypt, where the caliph al-Fa'iz had died, on July 23, 1160. His successor, chosen by Ibn Ruzzik, was a nine-year-old cousin of the dead caliph: he took the name al-'Adid, and would be the last of the Fatimid caliphs. Ibn Ruzzik also took the opportunity to renew his demands upon Usama, and again urged him to return. But Usama had had enough of Egypt and its intrigues; by 1160, at the age of sixty-five, with only his friends and immediate family to console him, he had probably had enough of just about everything.

At this ripe age Usama decided to undertake an obligation incumbent upon all able-bodied Muslims: the *hajj*, or pilgrimage to Mecca. From Syria, a lavish formal procession would normally depart south from Damascus during the month of pilgrimage and, picking up more groups of pilgrims on the way, pass through Transjordan to the west coast of Arabia and the holy cities of Mecca and Medina. In 1160, for example, Shirkuh, who was serving as Nur al-Din's governor of Damascus, led the pilgrimage. For reasons of his own, Usama did not join this procession, but took a different route, north through Iraq, meeting up with the hajj caravan that departed from Baghdad. On the way, he visited Mosul and was hosted by a companion serving there as vizier, to whom Usama offered some sage advice about spending too lavishly and too openly. After performing the pilgrimage to Mecca and Medina, Usama rejoined the Damascus caravan and returned to Syria.

By 1162, a reinvigorated Nur al-Din was eager to take the field against the Franks, and Usama joined him. It may be that Nur al-Din was motivated by cynical reasons, for in 1161, Ibn Ruzzik, Usama's old friend, had been killed by his amirs. Having formerly refused Ibn Ruzzik's request to join him in a campaign against the Franks, Nur al-Din may well have thought that, with Ibn Ruzzik dead and Egypt facing another crisis of leadership, the field was now open, and his activities against the Franks now could only benefit himself.

His goal was the key fortress of Harim, which lay on the borders of the principality of Antioch and the territory of Aleppo, and which the Franks had been using to harass the latter ever since they seized control in 1158.

Nur al-Din was to be disappointed at Harim. The campaign was a dismal failure, and he was obliged to lift his siege and retreat to Aleppo. He would encounter an even greater failure the following year, during an attack on Tripoli. At the foot of the mighty fortress of Crac des Chevaliers, Nur al-Din encountered a vastly reinforced Frankish army, its ranks swollen with Byzantine troops shipped to Tripoli by the emperor Manuel Comnenus. The Muslim army was thrown into disarray, and he barely escaped with his life.

Nur al-Din seems to have been shaken by this experience. He turned to a more ascetic lifestyle, and earnestly prepared his troops to regain their honor in the field. His revenge came in August 1164. His army, which might have included the sixty-nine-year-old amir Usama, captured the coveted fortress of Harim and inflicted a humiliating defeat on the Franks. Among the prisoners that Nur al-Din took that day were none other than the prince of Antioch, the count of Tripoli, the count of Edessa, and the Byzantine duke commanding the troops sent from Constantinople.

Among the Muslim amirs who distinguished themselves that day was Qara Arslan, lord of the remote fortress town of Hisn Kayfa in the province of Diyar Bakr in northern Iraq. In one of those unknowable moments that have now become commonplace in Usama's story, he decided to leave the court of Nur al-Din for that of Qara Arslan in Hisn Kayfa. Nur al-Din's turn to extreme asceticism was grating on Usama's nerves, to judge by some surviving poetry, and he may well have been worried by his bouts of illness and – despite his recent triumph – his run of bad luck in the field. Whatever the reasons, in 1164 Usama gave up Damascus for Qara Arslan's service in Diyar Bakr, where he would spend a decade doing that which would make him immortal: writing.

3

THE POET AND THE TOMB

On arrival in the province of Diyar Bakr in 1164, Usama entered the period of his life that is the most obscure to us now whilst, paradoxically, one of the most celebrated. On the one hand, he has left very little direct information about his decade of service to the amir Qara Arslan, except for a few anecdotes about hunting; other medieval sources similarly have little to tell us about these years, until Usama's death in Damascus in 1188. On the other hand, this is when Usama wrote the works that made him noteworthy both among his contemporaries and succeeding generations of literati: his topical anthologies, his poetry, and, above all, his collection of autobiographical anecdotes, the *Book of Learning by Example*. If we know anything at all about Usama directly, it emerges from this period of shadow.

DIYAR BAKR (1164–1174)

Some sense of Usama's new patron and setting can be reconstructed. The amir Qara Arslan belonged to a petty dynasty of Turcoman warlords, the Artuqids, who ruled over the region of Diyar Bakr from the end of the eleventh until the early fifteenth century. They began as independent warlords in Palestine, Syria, Iraq, and, finally, in the region of Diyar Bakr (which embraced the upper basin of the Tigris river system in present day south-eastern Turkey and northern Iraq). Although their early, further-flung possessions were lost to the empire-building Saljuq sultans, in Diyar Bakr, the Artuqids remained unchallenged. Amid, the principal city of the region, remained long outside their control, but the Artuqid amirs were, nevertheless, able to systematically fend off the ambitions of the Saljuq sultans and the atabeg Zangi by maintaining a united front against any claims on their territories. But Artuqid unity did not last forever, and by the time Usama left the court of Nur al-Din, they had, more or less permanently, divided into two rival lines: one based usually at Mayyafariqin, the other at Hisn Kayfa.

Hisn Kayfa, the domain of Usama's new protector, Qara Arslan, calls Shayzar to mind in its impressive situation. Looming over the Tigris atop a prodigious rocky outcrop, and surrounded on three other sides by ravines, the castle of Hisn Kayfa was practically impregnable. Its lower town, stretched before it along the banks of the river, was an important frontier post and commercial center. Here the septuagenarian Usama found quiet and, increasingly, isolation. As medieval frontier principalities go, Qara Arslan's amirate was comparatively tame. The most significant political event of his reign was his attempt to capture the city of Amid in 1163 – one of many such attempts – but the Artuqid troops were driven back. The most salient feature of Qara Arslan's regime, particularly in light of the long lifespan of the dynasty, was its change of attitude following the rise of Nur al-Din. For, by this time, the Artuqids, Qara Arslan foremost among them, had seen the wisdom of abandoning their old rivalries and become reliable allies of Nur al-Din.

For Usama, who had seen the heights that Cairo and Damascus could offer, Diyar Bakr was a terribly provincial place, "a lost corner of the world" (KI, 101 / 196). In the little information we have of his activities, one detects a certain restlessness. He certainly did not let the grass grow beneath him. In June 1166, we find him at Mayyafariqin; in August 1167, at Is'ird. Two months later, Qara Arslan died, and was succeeded by his son Muhammad, which Usama never mentions. The new lord of Hisn Kayfa may not have been on friendly terms with Usama but he still traveled freely. In May 1170, he was in Mosul, but, narrowly missing (perhaps intentionally) the arrival of his former patron Nur al-Din, had returned to Hisn Kayfa by December.

He is also known to have visited Irbid and to have returned to Is'ird (KA, *passim*). Qara Arslan had also granted Usama an Armenian village in the district of Balu, between Erzurum and Khilat in eastern Anatolia, which he visited and about which he composed a poem (*Diwan*, 159). During most, if not all, these visits, he was hosted and entertained by the elite: descendants of the Prophet, amirs, men of letters, and local notables. Had Usama not named them, many of these people would be utterly unknown. Whether these visits were connected to campaigns during Qara Arslan's poorly documented reign remains unknown.

Usama was not entirely alone in Qara Arslan's court. His son Murhaf joined him in Hisn Kayfa, or at least visited him; his brother Munqidh, himself the author of a (lost) chronicle, was living upstream in nearby Amid, and the two corresponded. In 1166, moreover, and much to his amusement, Usama was blessed with a daughter, whom he named Umm Farwa (*Diwan*, 273). But these few family relations were not enough to dispel the feelings of loneliness and solitude produced by old age, as he outlived more and more of his old companions and kin (*Diwan*, 302):

> They have breathed their last, and their loss was death to me.
> It is for me that one should weep, not for them.
> For I have outlived them, and I seem now like a man struck by
> paralysis in an endless desert.

LITERARY OUTPUT

Although Usama always found time to write poetry, his stay in Diyar Bakr offered him the first real period of calm since his early years at Shayzar. Here he composed the largest part of his works, only some of which have survived. Since only a few of these works are securely dated, it is difficult to construct even a relative chronology of his literary output. But we can, none the less, get some sense of his interests. Judging by the contents of the surviving works and by the titles of those lost to us, Usama specialized in the creation of miscellanies of verse and prose connected to a particular theme.

This sort of *adab*-anthology was one of the most common forms of literature in Usama's day, but he was fairly original in his selection of topics. He composed, for example, whole works devoted to castles and fortresses, rivers, dream visions, consolation, bearing loss, and exemplary women. One lost work, on youth and old age, was written for his father (who died in 1137), and so must have been one his earlier pieces; another, *Counsel to Shepherds*, was written before 1172. As medieval Muslim rulers often fancied themselves benign minders for a vulnerable, subject "herd," this title suggests that it falls into the "mirror for princes" genre of political advice and so was possibly intended for the prince Qara Arslan; it too may well have been an anthology. Two of his surviving works that certainly are anthologies give some sense of what the lost ones may have looked like and help us to see that anthologizing does not necessarily imply a lack of creative energy or originality.

The *Book of the Staff (Kitab al-'Asa)*, written in 1171 or 1172 is, as the title suggests, a collection of verse and prose selections devoted (more or less) to the subject of staves and walking-sticks, symbols, for Usama, of his increasing age and infirmity. The work includes narratives about famous historical staves such as those of Solomon or Moses, stories about staves from Usama's own life and times, and sundry lexicographical detours. The poems include selections from every age of Arabic poetry, from the giants of the pre-Islamic era to the classical versifiers of the Umayyad and Abbasid courts, to the more florid poets and poetasters of later times, including Usama and others of the Banu Munqidh.

Usama is best known for his "memoirs," but, properly speaking, the second of his surviving anthologies, *Dwellings and Abodes (Al-Manazil wa'l-Diyar)*, could claim to be his true masterpiece. A thick book in its printed edition, *Dwellings* is an immense and exacting analysis of the components of the *nasib*, or erotic prelude, of the classical Arabic ode. In the prelude, Arab poets traditionally described the abode of the beloved (either one's kin or one's lover) after they have departed. Haunted by dwelling-places abandoned, destroyed, or simply effaced by the passage of wind and time, the stark emotional landscape that the lovelorn poet confronts in the prelude sets the stage for the flood of memories of passions tasted and honor enflamed embraced by the full fury of the rest of the ode. In *Dwellings*, Usama organizes his work around the various symbols employed by the poets to evoke these places of memory and desire, citing example after example of poetic excerpts that, to his taste, have excelled at deploying them to their fullest.

And he, of all people, should know. And this is precisely what raises the work above his other literary gestures. For not only was he a poet, who could be expected to flourish verses by his or other hands on a given theme, not only was he a master of Arabic rhetoric, who could be expected to know an exquisite sample from a crass pastiche, but he was also a living example – perhaps the most famous – of the largely symbolic despondent lover that the poets had placed at the center of their preludes. Usama, as his contemporaries knew only too well, had genuinely and sincerely gazed upon the deserted traces of his own effaced abode high above the Orontes, and spent the remainder of his life wandering in mourning for his lost beloved kinsmen. In his introduction to the work, he explains his inspiration (MD, 3–4):

> I was moved to compile this book by the destruction that befell my land and my home. For Time has dragged its hem across them, serving thereby to obliterate them utterly. They became "as if they had not been inhabited yesterday," empty courtyards once full of life. Fate destroyed their buildings and killed their inhabitants. Their dwellings became as mere traces, and the joys found there became mere sorrow and care. I came upon my homeland after the earthquake had struck it, [as the poets say] "the first earth whose dirt touched my skin." But I did not recognize my home, nor the homes of my father and brother, nor the homes of my uncles and cousins and my family. I stood shocked, perplexed, seeking protection in God from the gravity of His trials, and His snatching back what He had granted of His blessings …
>
> Misfortunes had accumulated such that my tears could no longer flow. I was wracked with such moaning that the bow of my ribs was straightened. The vicissitudes of Time did not stop short of destroying our dwellings, sparing their inhabitants, but rather ended

them all together in the twinkling of an eye, or faster. Then disaster followed after disaster from that time and henceforth. And so I sought solace in compiling this book, and fashioned it as a keening for my homeland and beloved ones, even though it accomplishes nothing. Nevertheless, it is the furthest extent of my efforts. From God – may He be glorified and exalted – I beg recompense from what I have encountered in my life, my separation from my household and my kin, and my estrangement from hearth and homeland ...

I fashioned this book in sections, opening each section with material that suits my current plight, then offering material that better suits those whose hearts are light, so that the book should not be found to be all weeping and wailing, with nothing in it but relief for those in mourning. That said, the misfortunes of this world are like Death, which merely forbears, but never overlooks. For if today you are upright, tomorrow you will be overturned ...

To grasp this lesson is difficult, and to encompass it fully is not really possible. All I have tried to do is to collect that which cools the pangs of the heart and silences all disquiet apart. I offer my effusive apologies to anyone who should come across this work. Accepting them is something noble folk would not shirk.

Combining an encyclopedic understanding of centuries of Arabic poetry, a refined sense of the poet's art and a deep and touching melancholy from its first to last pages, *Dwellings* may be more of an embodiment of its author than even his "memoirs." It also represents Usama's earliest example of self-depiction. By constant reference to the manners of classical Arabic poetry (Time, dwellings, the vicissitudes of Fate), he used the lengthy introduction to create an image that was not just sympathetic to his contemporaries (and potential patrons), but one that placed him among the other Fate-struck wandering poets of a greater age.

The image appears to have stuck. Usama was viewed by his contemporaries as a master of high literary style, in particular of *badi'*, the ornate poetic mode of his age, so it was only a matter of time before Usama attempted to assemble a theoretical work devoted to the principles of this new style. His surviving treatise, the *Creator of High Style* (*al-Badi' fi'l-Badi'*) is very much a distillation of the conclusions and examples of earlier rhetorical masters. It is undated, but was probably composed in Diyar Bakr or in Damascus in his last years. Usama described the work thus (BB, 21–22):

> I have assembled in this book various things found scattered in the books of the old masters composed on the topic of poetic criticism and poetry's merits and faults. It is they who have the virtue of being innovators (*fa-la-hum fadilat al-ibtida'*), while I have merely the virtue of following them ... I assembled the best parts from those books and cited from them the best examples, in the hope that by including all that is excellent in them, my book may stand in their place.

Usama also devoted some of his time to pious works, although even his more topically "secular" works often contained reflections or comment that we would call "religious," such as Qur'anic commentary, Prophetic tradition, pious narratives, and so on. Among his explicitly "religious" works, Usama composed (we don't know when) a history of the battle of Badr, a famous victory of the Prophet and the early Muslim community against their pagan enemies in Arabia that is seen as a turning-point in Islam's sacred history. In Diyar Bakr, he also composed summaries of two longer works by his younger contemporary, the great Baghdadi scholar Ibn al-Jawzi (died 1200), devoted to the merits (*manaqib*) of the pious caliphs 'Umar ibn al-Khattab and 'Umar ibn 'Abd al-'Aziz, considered "Rightly Guided" exemplary leaders by many Muslims; accounts of their meritorious deeds were frequently collected and studied as guides to righteous conduct.

These religious works show a historical bent, an interest in the "Golden Age" of early Islamic history, and most of Usama's remaining works gave full vent to this interest. For example, he is credited with a continuation of the history of literary greats of the Arabo-Islamic world, started by the prolific literary scholar al-Tha'alibi (died 1038), a book on topography or geography, and two works referred to simply as "accounts of his family" and "accounts of his days" which may both be references to his "memoirs."

By the end of February, 1173, Usama passed into his eightieth Muslim year, a milestone significant enough for him to reflect in verse upon the costs of so long a life's journey (KI, 163/194):

When, at eighty, time plays havoc with my power of endurance,
I am chagrined at the feebleness of my foot and the trembling of my hand.
While I write, my script looks crooked,
Like the writing of one whose hands have shivers and tremors.
What a surprise it is that my hand is too feeble to carry a pen,
After it had been strong enough to break a lance in a lion's breast...
       And, full of complaint (KI, 164/195):
Destiny seems to have forgotten me, so that now I am like
An exhausted camel left by the caravan in the desert.
My eighty years have left no energy in me.
When I want to rise, I feel as though my leg were broken.
Sitting, I recite my prayers; for kneeling,
If I attempt it, causes pain.
This condition has forewarned me that
The time of my departure on the long journey has drawn nigh

Indeed it had. Within a year, Usama had left Diyar Bakr, startled out of his musings about old age by an invitation to move to his beloved Damascus, to the court of the legendary Saladin. It would be his last journey.

DENOUEMENT IN DAMASCUS (1174–1188)

Usama had first met Saladin back in 1154, when Saladin was only seventeen and still a retainer to his father Ayyub, who, with his brother Shirkuh, had come to Damascus to render service to Nur al-Din in Damascus. His rise in the twenty years that followed owes as much to Saladin's own ambition as to the strategic needs of Nur al-Din's fledgling principality. In 1163, Amalric, Frankish count of Ascalon and Jaffa, succeeded to the throne of the kingdom of Jerusalem. As king, Amalric's eyes turned to Cairo, still the capital of Fatimid Egypt, but now the scene of fearful factionalism within the palace and civil strife outside it. Wracked by unrest, the Fatimid caliphate was disintegrating.

Nur al-Din, too, was attentive to the situation in Egypt, and had sent his general, Shirkuh, to assist the Fatimid vizier in his bid to restore order. But Shirkuh quickly became embroiled in the local conflicts, and the vizier turned against him. Beset both by local rivals and a hostile Sunni army under Shirkuh, the vizier took the desperate step of appealing to Amalric for aid. But this solved none of his problems. On the contrary, in 1168, Nur al-Din again sent Shirkuh to Egypt to assist the vizier as he faced a Frankish assault. Having forced Amalric and his armies to withdraw, the victorious Shirkuh had the Fatimid vizier murdered and himself named in his place, only to die two months later. Shirkuh was succeeded by his nephew, Saladin, now a trusted amir in the service of Nur al-Din. The contradictions in such a position did not take long to manifest, and Saladin soon found himself poised to supplant Nur al-Din.

During Usama's first meeting with Saladin, Usama's own son Murhaf met and befriended him. The two grew to be close companions, and Murhaf later became a trusted amir in Saladin's army and a palace confidant. One can thus imagine how Usama attracted Saladin's interest. Murhaf, close to Saladin, will have mentioned his father, the venerable warrior-poet, vegetating in faraway Diyar Bakr. Saladin, entrenched in Cairo, his eyes set on Syria, may well have remembered the old amir who had served both the Fatimids and Nur al-Din and had connections in Cairo, Damascus, and throughout Syria. Usama, for his part, could hardly be called coy, for we find him firing off verse after unctuous verse congratulating Saladin on the military victories that marked his early years in Egypt.

Eventually, Usama's persistence was rewarded. On the death, in 1171, of the Fatimid caliph al-'Adid, Saladin dispensed with the formality of Fatimid allegiance and set about ruling Egypt openly, albeit nominally as Nur al-Din's servant. For example, he began minting coins with the Abbasid caliph's name on one side, and Nur al-Din's on the other; no one could accuse Saladin of being anything other than a good servant. However, disputes over Egypt's revenues and Saladin's increasingly independent behavior raised tensions with Nur al-Din, and it looked very much as if the two men would soon come to blows. Saladin was saved the prospect of marching against his old master when Nur al-Din died unexpectedly in Damascus on May 15,

1174. He now set his sights in earnest on his master's former possessions in Syria. By October, he had abandoned Cairo for a court closer
to the front lines in Damascus, where he would be better placed to
neutralize his foes among Nur al-Din's kin and former servants.

It was then that Usama was summoned to Damascus. The old man
was elated to be leaving provincial Diyar Bakr, having "exercised the
patience of a captive with his chains, and of a thirsty man held back
from water." As he would later describe it (KI, 165/196):

> Suddenly [Saladin] extricated me from the very teeth of calamities
> through his good will, transported me to his [court in Damascus]
> through his abundant benevolence, set right all that Time had inflicted
> upon me, and through his generosity put me in commission after I
> had been considered of no use by all on account of my old age ...
> His generosity left no desire in me which I wish to fulfill. I therefore
> spend my life praying for him, day and night ... May our community
> remain as it is, in an impregnable defense, thanks to his swords; and in
> a flourishing spring season, thanks to his liberality.

Springtime it may have seemed to a richly rewarded courtier like
Usama, but October 1174 brought a very bitter autumn indeed to
the kin and commanders of Nur al-Din. Potential resistance to Saladin lay in two areas: first in northern Iraq, base of Nur al-Din's two
nephews, Zangi, lord of Sinjar (not to be confused with the atabeg
Zangi of earlier times), and his brother Sayf al-Din Ghazi of Mosul,
and second in Aleppo and northern Syria, where Nur al-Din's young
son al-Salih had been taken for safekeeping by a group of his old commanders from Damascus. Damascus itself thus offered no resistance
to Saladin. To neutralize the threat from the princes of Iraq, Saladin
encouraged their existing disputes. As the brothers squabbled,
the field was left open in Syria, and Saladin spent the next several
months consolidating his hold, taking Homs, Hama, and Baalbek
before agreeing to a truce before the walls of Aleppo in 1175. After
this, Saladin left for Cairo but returned to Syria and northern Iraq
several times to campaign against the Franks, Armenians, and those
remaining Muslim amirs who opposed him. By summer 1183, only
Aleppo stood out, and it too fell, by treaty, on June 11. Saladin now

governed Egypt, most of Syria and northern Iraq. Only the Crusader principalities of the coast remained unconquered.

During this period of consolidation, Usama was enjoying his life's final flowering. While his son Murhaf accompanied Saladin on his campaigns, one imagines Usama, in Damascus, an old and scarred veteran, putting the finishing touches to his written works. Saladin seems to have accorded him some respect. According to one medieval historian, he frequently met Usama and treated him as a confidant, seeking his advice on matters of (what else?) *adab* and, above all, warfare: "When he was away from him while on campaign, he would write to him and recount the events and battles, demanding to know his advice in order to assuage his worries and resolve the difficulties that tormented him" (Abu Shama, *Rawdatayn*, 1997, 2:435). Saladin also richly rewarded Usama, granting him control over the revenues from the lands around the town of Ma'arrat al-Nu'man, ancestral lands of the Banu Munqidh in their heyday. Usama wrote of visiting Hama during this period, where he heard a story about nearby Ma'arat al-Nu'man. Otherwise, he seems not to have stirred from the city, which offered him the prospect of a placid and safe old age. "I am his guest," Usama later wrote in a panegyric to Saladin, "and the threatening hand is powerless to grasp he who enjoys the hospitality of the sultan" ('Imad al-Din, *Kharida*, 1951, 1:531).

INTELLECTUAL PURSUITS

Inactivity seems not to have troubled Usama, and he embraced the intellectual pursuits that Damascus had to offer, relishing the frequent contact with like-minded men. In his previous periods of residence, he had attracted some student following, and a later biographical note lists a number of prominent scholars who heard him lecture during his early and later years in the city (Ibn al-'Adim, *Bughya*, 1988, 3:1359). Just what Usama's specialty was is hard to say: the implication is that Usama transmitted Prophetic tradition, something that he certainly studied as a youngster and knew well, but was not really his *métier*. Certainly his contemporaries valued him as a source of what we would call more secular information, especially poetry. He was said to have a prodigious memory for Arabic verse, and was eagerly sought both for his own works and his ability to recite those of the old masters. His companions in these literary pastimes included some of the bright lights of Saladin's court, such as his vizier al-Qadi al-Fadil and his chief scribe 'Imad al-Din, both men of stellar literary achievement. We know that Usama sent a copy of his *Book of the Staff* to al-Qadi al-Fadil for their florid, punning correspondence was preserved by 'Imad al-Din as a model of epistolary style. 'Imad al-Din numbered Usama among Syria's most prominent poets and had heard of him as a poet and rhetorician even before coming to serve with Saladin, and eagerly hoped to meet him one day ('Imad al-Din, *Kharida*, 1951,1:499):

> Already at Isfahan, [the poet] al-'Amiri had recited to me those poems of [Usama's] that he retained. I wished for a very long time to make his acquaintance and, despite the distance that separated us, I would [as it were] watch the horizon to see if rain was imminent.

'Imad al-Din finally met Usama in Damascus in September 1175; the first of many such salons, which Murhaf and even Saladin himself (who enjoyed their company while playing chess) attended.

However, as long as Saladin remained the focus of Usama's courtly existence, none of this quiet pleasure could last. When Saladin took 'Imad al-Din and Murhaf with him on campaign, Usama wrote letters to them expressing his dismay and loneliness. When Saladin left Egypt, his dismay turned to despair as he was left, forgotten and ignored, in Syria. This was when, removed from the distractions of the court, Usama set to work, reflecting on his long life and its instructive episodes.

One of the products of this activity was Usama's *Kernels of Refinement (Lubab al-Adab)*. An anthology, like many of his earlier works, *Kernels* is a guide to proper social conduct. A manuscript of the work, dated to 1183, survives and was presented to Usama's son Murhaf in 1186. Like the *Book of the Staff*, it consists of diverse excerpts of Arabic poetry including Usama's own, pungent narratives, Qur'anic criticism, Prophetic tradition, and meandering autobiographical accounts. It is organized into chapters devoted to those features that Usama deemed crucial prerequisites for those seeking refinement and courtly poise – *adab par excellence*: political savvy, generosity, courage, immaculate manners, rhetorical style, knowledge of wise sayings and *bons mots*, and so on. Not just a book of advice, it is a blueprint for the ideal Muslim courtier in the age of the Crusades, but has received practically no attention from cultural historians.

It was probably also in Saladin's court that Usama compiled his anthology, or *Diwan*, of his own poetry. Although he was best known to his contemporaries for his compositions and his prodigious knowledge of the Arabic poetic heritage, his own collection seems to have been badly treated by history. Medieval sources attest that he compiled this anthology, that it was a favorite of Saladin's, and that it remained "in the hands of the people" well after his death (Ibn Khallikan, *Wafayat*, 1968, 1:196); but only two manuscripts of the *Diwan* are known to have survived, and the first was only noticed and edited in Egypt in 1953. Before then, we knew of Usama's poetry only through quotations in other works.

One should still be thankful for those quotations, for Usama's *Diwan* is not a comprehensive anthology of his entire poetic output, but rather a slender compilation in which one looks in vain for many of the poems and fragments cited in other works. His poetic *oeuvre* must have been far more substantial than that preserved in the *Diwan*. But then, Usama may never have intended the *Diwan* to be a complete archive. Rather, in keeping with his status as a master of his art and as a teacher, he may have seen it as a source-book of exemplary poetic style, as suggested by the format of one of the two surviving manuscripts. Typically, Arabic poems maintained a rhyme scheme based on the final sound of their lines, and were grouped accordingly. For example, all poems whose lines ended in the sound "*ab*" were grouped together and were said to "rhyme in the letter *b*." In collections, the usual practice was to arrange these groupings alphabetically, the poems rhyming in *b* preceding the poems rhyming in *t*, and so on. One of the surviving manuscripts of the *Diwan* (and the modern edition) is so organized. However, the other abandons this alphabetical rhyming system altogether and is arranged in chapters according to poetic mode: erotic verse, panegyric, elegy, and so on (only satirical verse seems – more or less – absent). A full Arabic ode, in all its glory, very frequently exemplified all these modes, and so, in this copy of the *Diwan*, Usama has no compunction about cutting up his odes into their various components and filing these segments in the appropriate chapters. For readers expecting Usama's *Diwan* to be a simple collection of his complete poems, one after the other, the result is something of a jigsaw puzzle or mosaic. But for Usama it is the poetic mode, not the poetry itself, which is important here.

This is not to say Usama's poetry fell on deaf ears. Saladin's fondness for it has been noted, and others agreed. Many included his poetry in their anthologies of literary greats; others boasted of owning a copy of his *Diwan*. Ibn 'Asakir, a former pupil and a historian of Damascus, considered his former teacher "the poet of the age" whose works were "sweeter than honey and to be savored more than slumber after a long period of waking." (Ibn 'Asakir, *Ta'rikh*, 1998, 1:90–91) On the whole, Usama's poetry bears all the hallmarks of his age: heavily ornate, almost baroque; using puns and wordplay to such a degree that his precise meaning often puzzles modern editors, not to mention modern readers. Usama especially enjoyed alluding to or even sampling from the old masters of classical Arabic poetry, such as Abu Nuwas or Abu Tammam. This was a style which, although common in his day, was nevertheless seen by some of his critics as unoriginal or even dishonest. He also tended to shy away from abstraction, so his poetry is often highly narrative in structure, which should endear it to historians more than it has. Like many of his peers, Usama often conducted correspondence in verse. Among others, his poetic exchanges with Ibn Ruzzik, the vizier of Egypt, were substantial and are well preserved, and are untapped evidence of the events and emotions surrounding the reign of Nur al-Din. For all that his contemporaries appreciated it, Usama's poetry has not found an equivalent modern following.

In addition to compiling his *Diwan*, Usama spent these latter days of solitude working on his *Book of Learning by Example* (*Kitab al-I'tibar*), often, and quite inaccurately, referred to as his "memoirs."

It survives in only one manuscript, found in the Escorial monastic library near Madrid, in a damaged and incomplete state. Nevertheless, it has been the subject of editions and translations since the nineteenth century. Usama began compiling anecdotes for the *Book of Learning* during his stay in Diyar Bakr, but it was only completed (if one can say it ever was) shortly before he died. He may well have been tinkering with it for over a decade.

For all the similarity it has with other works of Arabic literature, the *Book of Learning* is unique. It is startlingly autobiographical – although not alone in medieval Arabic letters in that respect – and charmingly chatty, dropping details of daily life in the author's day in a manner reminiscent of other literary collections of "rare anecdotes" or "table talk" that Usama himself would have enjoyed. It seems random, flitting from topic to topic much like Usama's other anthologies. But it is neither fully a "memoir" (no such genre existed at the time, anyway), a standard collection of light tales, nor the usual sort of topical reader. It is what its title says it is: a book of examples (*'ibar*) from which to draw lessons; its uniqueness lying in the intimate subjects of its examples.

Happily for historians (and biographers), Usama draws most of these lessons from his own long and varied life. Events from Usama's childhood and early life in Shayzar and his intrigues after his exile are all vividly recorded. The Banu Munqidh, the Franks, Egyptians, Syrians, men and women, and friends and foes from all walks of life populate its pages. Then there is hunting: so detailed are these sections that even today the zoological information they contain is a subject of scholarly controversy, with some of the species mentioned defying modern identification. Usama's musings on his past could be summed up in one idea: humanity's utter powerlessness in the face of the manifestation of God's will that he and his contemporaries called Fate. As we shall see later, the inevitability of God's will was one of the main ordering principles of Usama's world. No matter the person (or animal) or the context, it is God who chooses the time to enact His will and to cause success or failure, in defiance of expectation. A courageous warrior cannot overcome his fate, but anyone can survive any number of lethal blows if their time has not yet come. The time and circumstances of our end are not of our choosing: a hornet sting may kill a miller if God so decides, but a dog may save another man from a lion's attack. A Frank might be killed by one of Usama's kinsmen, then again, he might be taken by a (counter-crusading?) leopard. And, time and time again, true strength of character shines in what, to Usama, were unlikely places: in women, slaves, and even animals.

Since the inevitability of Fate was clearest in the fragility of the body and in death itself, Usama shows a rather obsessive interest in healing, medicine, and noteworthy cures: removing a carbuncle with a raw egg, curing a hernia by eating ravens, unusual blows in unusual locations, the horrors of Frankish medicine (and its possible virtues), and even a cure for the common cold (Indian melon); but despite humanity's weak attempts at staving off death, God's will was without remedy. The amount of medical observation in the *Book of Learning* is unusual, and probably indicates something about its author's state of mind: his musings may be the product of the inquiring mind of a warrior familiar with the body's supple limitations; then again, they may be the morbid fascinations of an ailing old man who often, in verse, begged for Time to release him.

If exemplary instruction is the ostensible theme of these "memoirs," they are also, like Usama in his last days, shot through with nostalgia and melancholy. The book is filled with tales of vanished companions, of early adventures, and above all, of Shayzar and his father, Murshid. Usama saw, in his father, all the quiet virtues of his day. "I know not," he would confess in a moment of self-criticism, "whether this was due to the fact that I was viewing him with love's eye... or whether my opinion of him was based on reality" (KI, 199/228). For all the advice, the battle tales, and the complaints of old age, the work is dominated by the young Usama admiring his father's falcons, chasing lions with him in the mountains of Shayzar, and fighting the Franks together amidst the stubborn rocks and forested gullies of the homeland to which, as to childhood, he could never return.

Usama died in Damascus on Thursday, November 17, 1188, at the astonishing age of 93, just over a year after Saladin had reconquered

Jerusalem and turned the tide of the Frankish occupation. The last image we have comes, unsurprisingly, from his *Book of Learning*. He is ailing and alone in Damascus, his patron and his beloved son virtually a world away (KI, 163/195):

> Enfeebled by years, I have been rendered incapable of performing service for the sultans. So I no more attend their courts and no longer depend upon them for my livelihood ... for I realize that the feebleness of old age cannot stand the exacting duties of service, and the merchandise of such a very old man cannot be sold to an amir. I have now confined myself to my own house, therefore, taking obscurity as my by-word.

As a close record of his last days, *The Book of Learning by Example* shows us that, however he might have been known to his contemporaries, whether as great warrior or peerless courtier, Usama ibn Munqidh lived his last moments as a grey and bent old lion, summoning the poetry of a youth ever itself unsummonable.

4

ORDER AND CHAOS

Most people who have heard of Usama ibn Munqidh know him through his famous "memoirs," which are themselves best known for their pointed observations of the Franks and medieval Muslim society. Very few realize that Usama wrote quite a bit more than his memoirs, and that a fair amount of his other work survives. Even fewer realize that, in these surviving works, for all that he wrote about Franks and others, he is equally revealing of himself: few figures in medieval Islamic history have laid bare their soul to the extent that Usama ibn Munqidh has. That is, no doubt, part of his appeal to modern readers, since the hearts and souls of most medieval people are utterly closed to us. What are the cultural categories in which Usama ordered his world? His poetry and autobiographical writings appear to be a perfect source from which to answer this question.

Appearances can be deceptive. In Usama's poetry – much of it precisely dated – in the autobiographical anecdotes included in some of his poetic anthologies, and, above all, in his memoir-like *Book of Learning by Example*, it is undoubtedly true that we possess a rare archive of one medieval individual's mind. However, such texts are neither straightforward documents, nor transcripts of conversations or interrogations, such as those other historians have used to access the views of the cosmos held by their subjects. Rather, they are deeply artificial, in the sense that they are products of the artifice of a master of his art, entrenched in the conventions and rules and expectations of a centuries-old Arabic tradition that governed what one could write about and how one could best write about it.

Usama's poetry, for example, tempts us to believe it as a source for understanding his emotions and motives. But such potential is severely curtailed when we take into account how much poetic convention militated against any explicit and frankly candid displays. Thus, when we read a poem like this, we might assume that Usama was stung by a spurned love at some point in his youth (*Diwan*, 100):

> What does desire need of a captive heart?
> It merely remembers the lover, the togetherness, and it yearns.
> It has sufficient quantities of desire already in it,
> Enough for it is the longing it has already amassed.
> Every time he sees a group together
> He soars with the joy of love and yearns in passion, and moans
> Even the rebuker mourns with him in pity
> And the jealous one sees in him what he wishes.
> Woe unto he who grows accustomed to a burning passion
> And abundant cares that beset one at night.
> O time when we were together! Still does
> The love flow, even though our dwelling-place be far away.
> Warn lovers that their dwelling is remote:
> As they approach it, they will start to gnash their teeth.
> I was wrong to think I could endure after you
> But my thoughts about you were perfect.

But then again, the poem could be nothing more than a one-off, the sort of thing that, by convention, poets were expected to write, in the sort of language they were expected to use. Even the nature of the relationship mourned in the poem is indeterminate: in the original Arabic, the beloved is described in a fittingly formal and anonymous masculine plural; a woman, man, or a group could be intended. Are these Usama's emotions, or the stock sentiments of literary convention? Whilst, like all good poets, Usama played with the conventions to show his originality, the candor that biographers need is hard to come by.

We are on only slightly safer ground with Usama's autobiographical writings. Here, conventions of genre and expression also apply. Both the *Book of Learning* and Usama's other works with autobiographical content are, above all, works of *adab*, of *belles-lettres*. Their chief goal is to entertain and admonish, not to relate truths about Islamic society in the age of the Crusades; historians who accept Usama's anecdotes, jokes and twice-told tales as truth do so at their peril. But perhaps the greatest obstacle to candor in Usama's prose is Usama himself, for, in the autobiographical anecdotes that he has left us, we are dealing not so much with Usama as with the particular image that he wished to leave for posterity. As we have seen, his "first person" report of the political intrigues in the Fatimid court in Cairo differs rather markedly from the way other chronicles describe the same events – notably with regard to his role in the plot against the vizier Ibn al-Sallar. We are left not with a historical personage so much as with a literary character, created by the historical Usama.

For all that, Usama's very artifice can betray his preoccupations, and his prose works are valuable for anyone seeking to get a glimpse of his mentality. It is not so much his direct statements about himself that are revealing, but the casual asides, the language he chooses to use, the ticks and wrinkles, even the omissions that show us what constituted his sources of anxiety and pleasure. Granted, any exercise using such sources is bound to be experimental, but even a cursory read of his anecdotes reveals a complex inventory of Usama's cultural baggage. What follows is an exploration of only a few of the principal items.

GOD'S WILL AND THE VICISSITUDES OF TIME

The reader quickly realizes that destiny was a major preoccupation for Usama. Like many literate men of his day, he liked to use the terms Fate (*dahr*) and Time (*zaman*) to express himself on the subject, keeping to the themes and favorite expressions of the ancient pre-Islamic poets. As mentioned earlier, the inevitability of one's private destiny is the main theme of the *Book of Learning*, which is intended to provide instructive examples of the whims of Fate, or rather the whims of God. For, by Usama's day, the Arabs had become monotheists, and the power of Fate merged very nicely with the omnipotence of God. For Usama, writing about Fate and Time and

Destiny was code for writing about God's will – and perhaps the other way around.

Because the inescapable nature of God's will is the main theme of the *Book of Learning by Example*, it is almost hardly worth mentioning as a concern: the very subject of the book obliged him to go on and on about it. Nevertheless, the fact that he *does* go on and on about God's will, that the theme turns up his other works, and was such a pervasive part of the medieval Islamic culture around him makes it worth noting, at least when we spare an eye for Usama's particular understanding of it.

Muslims in the Middle Ages adhered to an unshakeable belief in the overpowering might of God. But this raises serious issues about the ability to exercise free will: something Islamic theologians argued passionately over. As in all other monotheistic faiths, the issue hinges on salvation. Since God is omnipotent, we make our choices, meritorious or sinful, because He allows us to do so. But can we be fairly judged for our sins if we had no independent choice in committing them? If God pre-ordained all our deeds, good or bad, how can He be considered just in condemning sinners to Hell? Is He not the author of these deeds?

By Usama's era, the issue had long been settled in God's favor. Theologians were able to argue that God Himself created, at the very moment of the deed in question, the power for us to act, yet we still acquired the ramifications of our sins, and we were still to be judged if we were ever persuaded by the slanderous whispers of Satan. By Usama's day the vast majority of Muslims were predestinarians, striving to live good lives in the way God willed them to. For Usama, his belief in God's omnipotence manifested itself not so much in resignation as in wonder: to him, God's plan is inscrutable. His deeds and motives are mysterious, and, as Usama liked to say, He is "worthy of admiration" for the wonders of His creatures and the inevitability of His decrees. Some of Usama's sentiments are rooted directly in the Qur'an: God determines the length of life and fixes the hour of death; in His hand are all good things and He is all-powerful. He determines destinies and brings all things to pass. Other such musings on the power of God's will seem to come from direct observation: God decrees the safety of one group of Muslim soldiers by making their enemies over-cautious yet He allows another to be surprised by Franks through an execution of His will; a valiant horseman dies, but it was nothing but the ending of his predetermined days; survival from a wound is due to what God had seen fit to execute, just as the wound itself was in accordance with what He decreed; a patient afflicted with dropsy may die under a surgeon's knife, but another, stabbed in the stomach by a drunkard, may find himself suddenly cured. Above all, God grants victory and takes it away as He pleases, and there is a certain logic to what follows from such a belief. If God is the true source of any victory, it stands to reason, as Usama says, that holding aloof from battle no more delays one's fate than bravery hastens it and if only men would open their hearts to God, they would see this basic truth. Usama even offered himself as living proof of this inescapable conclusion. When one's days are over, courage and strength are of no avail. Organization and planning, troop numbers and supporters are irrelevant. "Fate," he concludes, "is an impregnable fortress" (KI, 147/177).

Even in the realm of laudable personal qualities, it is the Creator of these qualities, more than their human bearers, that is praised. Thus, the courage of a Sudanese soldier who audaciously flees from his pursuers, an "amazing thing (*'ajib*)" as Usama calls it, is an example of God's ability to determine our days (KI, 9/33–34). And the honor of the Banu Munqidh women, who would rather die fighting than allow themselves even to be touched by Nizari heretics, was an example of the remarkable qualities God created in women (KI, 123–26/153–55). And bad qualities may lead to bad choices, which bring down an equally wicked fate, as in the injustices of the Fatimid court during Usama's tenure there; injustices condemned by God Himself (KI, 21/47).

If Usama adhered to the fatalism of his times, it was not unnuanced. His ideas stem from pious observance of Qur'anic teachings, and are utterly in keeping with a prevailing but unarticulated concept of a transcendent, all-powerful, and all-merciful God. But more than ninety years of life experience meant that Usama could not refrain from enjoining his readers to prepare well when going to battle or the hunt, and from sharing a few trade secrets. As much as God may bring victory, Usama believes that it is safer in serious matters like warfare and hunting to hedge one's bets and not leave everything up to Him. One should hold one's lance in such a way when riding and one should always inspect the outfit of one's horse, for even a small flaw may prove crucial; inspiring awe through stratagems and ruses doesn't hurt your chances of victory; and above all, maintain reason, for the absence of reason – a quality praised by the intelligent and the ignorant alike – results always in error and failure.

Such advice may seem to contradict the notion that victory comes from God alone, and it must be said that if Usama was a fatalist, he was no theologian. He found his own compromise; one that allowed him to work to increase his chances for a just fate when it came, yet at the same time to retain a belief in an all-powerful and often inscrutable God. For Usama, human choices worked hand in hand, in unknowable ways, with God's decree to bring about a particular result. You can find your way through the desert using the stars in the heavens as a guide, but only if God's help accompanies you (KI, 13/37); a Bedouin guide might be clever enough to use sparks from a flint to attract the attention of a party gone astray, but it was God's kindness that allowed this to happen (KI, 13/38). Injustice and ingratitude have dire consequences, but only God's decree will determine what those consequences might be (KI, 29/55).

USAMA'S ISLAM

The power of God's will being what it is, Usama had very clear concerns about how to live his life in a way that was most pleasing to Him. This, of course, is true for any believer, and it is typical of the time that Usama was especially concerned about proper religious behavior, and, for various reasons, less concerned with religious teachings. At any rate, Usama was not given to theological discussion in his writings, but his asides about personal pious conduct are revealing of his religious beliefs.

First, the basics. Usama was a Muslim, but what *kind* of Muslim? Shi'ite or Sunni? The need to ask such a question indicates how little he reveals about the religious dimensions of his world, at least of the sort of hard and fast details that historians like to have. In the absence of any explicit information about Usama's religious beliefs, historians and biographers have had either to skirt the issue or fill in the gaps themselves. Surprisingly, this has led to the more or less prevailing (but incorrect) conclusion that Usama was a Shi'ite, presumably on the grounds that he admires 'Ali (KI, 173/205, 177/208–209), the cousin of the Prophet Muhammad and the first of the legitimate religious leaders (*imams*) recognized, by Shi'ites, as having succeeded the Prophet at his death. Moreover, the Banu Munqidh had a history of cooperation with Shi'ite dynasties in the area, in particular with the Fatimids in Egypt. Usama's service to the Fatimid caliphs, some would say, would be in keeping with his allegedly Shi'ite beliefs.

But none of this is very good evidence for one man's religious convictions. On the one hand, Sunnis also revere 'Ali, considering him one of the "Rightly Guided" caliphs of Islam's earliest generation, whom all Muslims should look up to as a model. On the other hand, the Fatimids employed many non-Shi'ites: indeed, it is safe to say that the majority of people working for the caliphs, including military men like Usama, were Sunni Muslims. The only clear evidence of Usama's Shi'ism is a quotation, in a lost Shi'ite history, from an eyewitness who names Usama as a Shi'ite who hid his beliefs (practicing *taqiyya* or precautionary dissimulation) for the sake of safety in a predominantly non-Shi'ite world (al-Dhahabi, *Ta'rikh al-Islam*, cited in Derenbourg, *Vie*, 1889, 602–603):

> Yahya ibn Abi Tayyi' mentions [Usama] in his *History of the Shi'ites*, saying: "My father related to me the following: 'I met him a number of times. He was an Imami Shi'ite, sound in his beliefs except that he used to conceal his orientation and exhibit *taqiyya*. He had abundant wealth and he used to help out the Shi'ites, being kind to the poor and giving to the notables.'"

This is hard to reconcile with the evidence of Usama's own works. It is especially difficult to believe that a Shi'ite, even a dissimulating one, would compose, as we saw in chapter 3, a work devoted to the merits of the caliph 'Umar ibn al-Khattab, whom Shi'ites revile as a usurper. Derenbourg thought this simply indicated that he had converted to Sunnism in Diyar Bakr, but there is no other reference to such a major change to corroborate this theory. Easy answers to questions of medieval religion are hard to come by, and the evidence of Usama's Shi'ism is, at best, ambiguous. Perhaps it is safest to assume that Usama was a Sunni Muslim, who, like many of his day, had what were called "acceptable Shi'ite tendencies" and also a more than passing association with Shi'ite regimes. But such labels only get us so far into understanding Usama's concerns about his relationship with God. We have no information at all about which school (if any) of Islamic law he followed, for example. We are little better off when we observe what he thought was good Muslim behavior. His religious devotions were not something he wrote about at length, either because he didn't practice them much, or because he didn't think they merited discussion. Nevertheless, he does comment on them from time to time, as well as on the devotional activities of others, and, if nothing else, it is possible to construct from these references a picture of the sorts of things that Usama found laudable in a Muslim, none of which is terribly unexpected. Many of his religious values would, then as now, be considered questionable by some strict interpreters of Islam, but Usama's religious life was wholly in line with most other Muslims of his time.

In Usama's mind, religion was almost inseparable from its practice. In praising the piety of his grandmother, for example, Usama claimed that she was "one of the most virtuous among Muslims, following the strictest paths of faith, fastidiousness, fasting, and prayer" (KI, 126–127/156). Likewise, he noted that a Frankish boy who converted to Islam seemed to be sincere, "judging by what he showed in the practice of prayer and fasting" and expressed some astonishment when the boy reverted to Christianity "after having practiced Islam with its prayers and faith" (KI, 130/160).

Praying and fasting, the *qiyam wa-siyam* of the sources, seem to be what Usama most associates with Islam, and these two Islamic ritual practices appear to have dominated his religious life as well as that of his peers. Usama and his companions paused to pray whilst chasing bandits, and even when hunting. Muslims, then as now, were enjoined to pray five times a day, and Usama has left anecdotes in which he mentions praying in at least one of each of the required prayer times. Whether he did so every day of his life is another matter. He famously complained, in a poem, about the pain it caused him to pray in his old age, and, when traveling, he shortened and combined his prayers, as Islamic law allowed. When the young Usama had to stop to pray during the hunt, it was a bit of a bore: he admits, on one occasion, to rushing through his prayers while his father was still absorbed, hoping to get back to the chase before his father could prevent him (KI, 126/155).

Fasting, too, is enjoined upon all Muslims, particularly during the holy month of Ramadan. But Usama had particular experience with voluntary fasts outside the mandatory Ramadan fasting. Such fasting was deemed especially virtuous, and was, for Usama, the mark of a true devotee. His father, for example, fasted daily (KI, 192/222), and obliged Usama to fast with him for a few days during the month of Rajab, a common but not mandatory devotional practice. Usama obliged of course, but longed to go hunting to take his mind off of his hunger (KI, 223/256). Nowhere, however, did he see such laudable fasting as with a learned ascetic sheikh, Muhammad al-Busti, whom he met while living in Hisn Kayfa. Al-Busti occupied a cell adjoining a mosque in the town, and Usama would visit him frequently to learn from him. "He would fast daily," Usama related, "drink no water, eat no bread and no kind of cereals. He would break his fast with two pomegranates or a bunch of grapes or two apples. Once or twice a month he would eat a few mouthfuls of fried meat." He was, according to Usama, "a learned ascetic, the like of whom I have never seen nor heard" (KI, 172/204).

PIOUS EXEMPLARS AND THE MIRACULOUS

Usama's father remained his closest religious role model. If he chafed occasionally under the ritual strictures imposed on him, later in life he praised his father's humble devotions. In addition to his penchant for fasting, Usama's father was recognized as a leader of prayer, and Usama recorded a touching vignette in which his father is seen leading Usama's grandmother in prayer in one of the private rooms in Shayzar. But it was his father's love of the Qur'an that stayed with Usama. Like his father before him, Usama's father was devoted to reciting the Qur'an, copying it, studying it and teaching it to his sons. As has been mentioned, when Usama's father died, he asked to be buried with his head upon one of the Qur'ans he had transcribed, and he was famed for his elegant calligrapher's hand. Even hunting, Usama tells us, was, for his father, exercise aimed at increasing his ability to memorize sacred scripture. To his last days, Usama continued his father's daily practice of reading portions of the Qur'an, preferring to stay up late rather than let a day pass devoid of quiet contemplation of God's word (KI, 20/45, 53/81, 127/156, 192/222).

In general, any elevated expression of personal austerity or devotional stricture was morally commendable in Usama's eyes. The men and women that seemed closest to God were those who fasted most, prayed most, and devoted their time to the Qur'an. There were also those who did without and faced personal rigors in God's name: lived lives of poverty, wore coarse wool, fought against infidels, or stuck to their beliefs no matter the cost. Such admirable people might be relatives, like Usama's father or brother (whom he commemorated as a great warrior of the faith). But they might also be non-Muslims, such as a Coptic patriarch he saw while living in Cairo. This man was thrown into prison and humiliated, but never gave in to the Fatimid vizier's demands upon him to break his religious law (LA, 72–73). As much as Usama could admire religious conviction of this kind, he found such pious behavior on the part of non-Muslims to be a little troubling (KA, 326–327/119):

> I went on pilgrimage to the tomb of John the Baptist – peace be upon him! – at a village called Sebaste in one of the sub-districts of Nablus. When I had performed my prayers, [I saw] a partially closed door, so I opened it and entered and [saw there] a church in which there were about ten old [Christian] men. Their heads were bared

and looked like carded cotton. They were facing east and had at their breasts staves topped by curved cross-bars the width of their chests. They propped themselves upon them while in front of them an old man recited to them. I saw there a sight that moved my heart but also grieved me and made me lament that I had never seen exertions like theirs among the Muslims.

Usama was later relieved of such anxieties when he encountered his first group of Sufis, Islamic mystics whose path to Islam involved rigorous devotional exercises and self-denial. In Damascus, his patron Unur invited him to visit the city's first Sufi lodge (KA, 327/119):

We entered it, and I did not think there was anyone there, but lo! There were around one hundred prayer-mats, on each one a Sufi exuding tranquility, his humility apparent. What I saw there of them gladdened me and I praised God – May He be glorified and exalted! – that I saw in the Muslims exertions greater than those of those priests [in Sebaste]. I had not before that time seen Sufis in their house nor did I know anything of their practice.

For Usama, non-Muslims might have piety, but they could never possess religious truth. For that, one had to attend to those Muslim men whom God had singled out as holy. Usama never calls the holy men he visited "Sufis;" this name he reserved for the organized mystics he met in Damascus, but they did share many ascetic practices popularly associated with Sufism. If, in Usama's mind, they were not Sufis, they were at least renunciants, men whose extreme acts of devotion and self-denial made them closer to God and even, in Usama's mind, capable of miracles. They included a man named Jarrar, who lived at a mosque near Shayzar and whom Usama used to visit for "blessings" (*baraka*), a key concept in Islamic attitudes toward the holy. So far as Usama tells us, this Jarrar did not himself perform miracles, but he did receive a staff from another ascetic that miraculously made him invisible to the Franks (KA, 235–237/116). Another such ascetic from Shayzar, Hasan, was also miraculously saved when God blinded him to a Frankish army storming the mosque he was praying in (KI, 91–92/121–122). Sometimes, the miracles border on parlor tricks, as with a holy man who produced a missing marriage contract from a package of sweets (KI, 170/202). For these true "friends of God," nothing was impossible. Even Usama, for all his self-acknowledged sins, believed that, when he was lost and fleeing his enemies in the deserts north of Egypt, he was saved by nothing less than an angel sent from on high (KI, 93/123).

But it was in dreams that true miracles tended to happen, where even the Prophet himself could visit the faithful and offer them succor. Usama was deeply attached to the power of dreams. In addition to his many anecdotes about dreams in his surviving works, he also devoted a separate work to the theme, now unhappily lost. Dreams of prophets and holy men were the preferred method of communication between the human and the divine. In them, figures like the Prophet Muhammad could offer guidance, admonitions, and information that might otherwise be secret. For example, a former prisoner encountered by Usama was able to escape from a dungeon in Armenia when the Prophet revealed the way in a dream (KI, 94/123). Another man claimed to have been cured of a tumor by seeing 'Ali in a dream; 'Ali cured another dreaming man of paralysis. And it was apparently not uncommon for poor men to make demands of a prince by claiming the Prophet had ordered them to do so in a dream, as Usama twice mentions (KI, 175–178/205–209).

The blessings that Usama sought from visiting ascetics and holy men outlived the lives of their human vessels. Sanctity, in Usama's world, lingered in concrete places, readily accessible for all to acquire through pilgrimage. Every Muslim is enjoined to perform the *hajj*, the pilgrimage to the holy city of Mecca, once in his or her lifetime, and Usama dutifully fulfilled this obligation. But he also made pilgrimages to other Muslim holy cities, like Jerusalem, and to lesser holy sites and tombs associated with pious figures both famous and obscure. When he visited Jerusalem, he prayed in the al-Aqsa Mosque, even though the Franks had turned it into the headquarters of the Knights Templar. His friends among that order allotted a certain amount of space for him to do so, something they probably did for any Muslim guest of a certain status (KI, 134–135/163–164). He also visited other places "where one can pray and expect blessings (*baraka*)," including the nearby Dome of the Rock and, in 1138, the Dome of the Chain. He was taken around these sites by a local pilgrims' guide of his acquaintance, who showed him the sites and told him bits of lore about them (KA, 234–235/115–116). It was around this time that he visited Sebaste and the tomb of John the Baptist, a figure venerated by Muslims and Christians alike. Even when on official business, as when the Fatimids sent him to Syria to raise troops, he took the opportunity to stop and pray at a site identified with the Cave of the Seven Sleepers (mentioned in the Qur'an) probably a site in the ancient Nabatean city of Petra in present-day Jordan. *Baraka* was not something one should casually pass by (KI, 15/39).

To readers today, Usama's fondness for dream-miracles and tomb visits may seem oddly out of place in a man who claimed to love reason and to admire strict observers of Islam. Indeed, to many Muslims, medieval and modern, such beliefs and practices conflict with what they deemed to be proper belief. But for Usama, and for millions of other Muslims, there was nothing impious in them. The Qur'an itself provides a model for dream-miracles, depicting Abraham, Joseph, and even the Prophet Muhammad himself receiving guidance from dreams. As for non-canonical visits to holy men or their tombs, there was as much to support such practices in Usama's day as there was to denigrate them. The great Muslim theologian al-Ghazali (died 1111), for example, wrote an influential defense of visiting holy sites.

Some practices were, for Usama, outside the pale of proper Muslim conduct. The commander al-Yaghisiyani was especially likely to exceed Islamic limits of morality in his martial zeal, murdering disobedient servants in ghoulish ways, roughing up prisoners, and even imprisoning Christians and Jews, who are, according to Islamic law, protected from such a fate. Usama could do nothing except pray to God to forgive him his excesses (KI, 159/189). Astrology, too, was something that Usama was never able to integrate fully into his religious world. His father's penchant for reading the heavens has been noted, and Usama found such behavior strange, even flawed, in a pious man. When he later wrote about the cataclysmic events he witnessed in Fatimid Cairo, he noted that the vizier 'Abbas had a love of astrology that blinded him to good counsel and ultimately spelled his doom.

Such belief in the power of the heavens smacked of vanity and fruitless human attempts to second-guess God's design. For Usama, this was only slightly less wicked than sorcery, itself a satanic distraction, a womanly and bestial pastime, judging from this unusually eerie account of Shayzar's resident witch by a local man, which Usama quotes in his *Book of Learning* (KI, 122–123/152):

> I went at night to the town, desiring to go into my home … as I approached town, I saw among the tombs in the moonlight a creature that was neither human nor animal. I halted at a distance from it and was frightened by it. Then I said to myself, "What is this fear from a mere single object?"… I advanced, step by step, while I could hear some singing and a voice emanating from that being. When I was close by it, I jumped over it, holding my knife in my hand, got hold of it and behold! It was [a woman named] Burayka with her hair spread all over, riding on a reed and neighing and roaming among the tombs. "Woe unto you," said I, "what are you doing here at this hour?" "I am performing sorcery," she replied. I said "May God abominate you, your sorcery and your art from among all arts!"

For Usama, his daytime visits to the tombs of holy men to pray or to receive blessings was a laudable act of personal piety, while the witch Burayka's nocturnal wanderings among the tombs of Shayzar smacked of necromancy. Such a distinction tells us much about what separates religion from magic for Usama; it also reveals a good deal about his views on women.

WOMEN'S HONOR

Usama lived in a hyper-masculine milieu, in which the social worlds of elite men took precedence over any competing world on offer, save that of God Himself. Women were an important part of that milieu, but only in carefully circumscribed roles and arenas. Women who sought power outside those arenas, like the witch Burayka, tended to be socially and morally marginalized.

Women's social and moral roles in Usama's world hinged upon the concept of honor: male anxieties about honor necessarily created rules about female honor. Honor was inextricably connected to descent: bloodlines were expected to be pure. An honorable man knew who both his parents were, and they conceived and raised him ideally as a married couple. Men revered female sexual honor in their own households and guarded it fiercely. Nothing could be more humiliating than to be a bastard, the son of an illicit sexual relationship. Men were willing to go to all sorts of lengths to prove their legitimacy, and any intimation of sexual impropriety among one's womenfolk was squashed quickly and definitively. Anything less dishonored a woman and by extension, her male kinsmen (KI, 15/39–40).

Truly virtuous women, it followed, tried to avoid situations where their honor might be impugned, or even where wagging tongues might suggest it. In Usama's world, virtuous women avoided strangers and public life (KI, 29–30/55), especially if unaccompanied. They wore modest dress and stayed out of trouble. They were rewarded for producing legitimate children, for adding grace and beauty to their household, and for their loyalty to their husband and his family. Muslim men were allowed to have more than one wife, but Usama is very reticent about this, and only mentions men having concurrent wives on one or two occasions. Though permitted, polygamy was probably not actively pursued in Usama's circles, at least not with the gusto that popular stereotypes about "the harem" would imply. Elite women could either hope to influence things quietly behind the scenes, or gain a reputation for piety and good works. And Islamic law technically accorded Muslim women some scope for inheritance and property ownership. But, so far as Usama reveals to us, the real lives of the women he knew were far more restricted than those of men.

With values such as these, it followed that younger women were socially favored over older. Older women were valued more for their wisdom and their ability to publicly shame younger men with emotional pleas and harangues than for anything else. It was older women who gave Usama useful advice, publicly mourned at funerals, nursed children and raised them and doted on them, and generally skulked about the edges and shadows of his world, quietly keeping it running while men followed their own rules, hunting and fighting.

When bandits and horse thieves wanted to travel unmolested, they dressed as old women (LA, 193; KI, 43/71). One can therefore understand the grief of a woman who, upon losing both her sons to al-Yaghisyani, succumbed to the realization that there was nothing left the amir could do to her (KI, 158–159/189).

An illuminating example of the male anxieties surrounding women's lives in Usama's world is the story of a wife of his uncle Sultan, apparently a local woman. He never mentions her name (as he almost never does for any woman), only describing her as "a woman of noble Arab origin." It seems that, when she was still living with her father, someone had described her to Sultan, who took an interest. But it was hardly suitable for the lord of Shayzar to go about making inquiries personally, so – note the detail – he sent an old woman of his household to meet and evaluate her. The old woman came back full of praise and delight, and Sultan married the woman without, as was customary, having seen her face. So enthusiastic had the old woman been about the bride's qualities that, in Usama's opinion, she had been bribed or met someone else, for the new wife turned out to be both ugly and mute. Sultan paid her the dowry required by Islamic law and sent her back to her father's home. For him, this was the honorable thing to do. But Sultan's unwanted wife tested his sense of honor on one other occasion, Usama tells us. During an attack on Shayzar and the vicinity, a Frankish army took many prisoners, including this woman. When Sultan learned this, he arranged to pay her ransom. The issue at hand was honor; hers, and thus, Sultan's: "I shall not let a woman whom I had married and who had unveiled herself before me stay in the captivity of the Franks" (KI, 71/100).

The Franks often turn up as the principal foil for Usama's comments on women's virtue. For Usama, the Franks are barbaric, little better than animals. This has almost nothing to do with the fact that they are Christian, for Usama was familiar with Christians and happy to give them credit where credit was due. What placed the Franks dangerously far from the limits of humanity was their lack of culture. For Usama, this Frankish cultural malady was most manifest in one symptom above all others: how they treated their women. "The Franks," Usama tells us, "lack all sense of shame or jealousy." He is astonished to note that a

Frankish man might leave his wife in public not merely alone, but alone with another man. He recounts a story in which a Frank comes home to discover his wife in bed with another man. When he politely asked the man what he was doing, the man replied he had merely come in to take a nap. As for the wife, well, it was her bed and she was entitled to sleep in it, too. The Frank let the interloper go with a stern warning. "Such was for the Frank," Usama concludes, clucking his tongue with distaste, "the entire expression of his disapproval and the limit of his jealousy" (KI, 135–136/164–165).

Franks were not only overly permissive of their women, and doltish when it came to their wiles, they were also positively childlike in their utter shamelessness of the body, male, and especially female. Any place where Franks and Muslims might peaceably mix was thus fraught with the potential for a clumsy Frank to break taboos. It didn't help to hear stories like this one, told by Salim, the bath attendant at Shayzar (KI, 136–137/165):

> I once opened a bath [in another town] to earn my living. A Frankish knight came to this bath. The Franks disapprove of wearing a towel around one's waist while in the bath, so this Frank ... pulled off my towel and threw it away. He noticed that I had recently shaved off my pubic hairs, so ... he stretched his hand over my groin and said, "Salim, good! By the truth of my religion, do the same for me." Saying this, he lay on his back and I found that in that place the hair was like his beard, so I shaved it off. Then he passed his hand over the place and, finding it smooth, he said, "Salim, by the truth of my religion, do the same to the *dama*" ... referring to his wife ... So [after a servant brought her in] I shaved all that hair while her husband was sitting looking at me. At last he thanked me and handed me the pay for my service.

Such comic accounts of the "manners and customs" of the Franks have made Usama's *Book of Learning* a perennial favorite among undergraduates, but the accounts are almost certainly a bit *too* comic, and should be seen as jokes rather than accurate accounts of Frankish life. Nevertheless, they do allow us to see how important female honor and chastity were for Usama, and how they were linked to his own worries. For what better way to belittle one's foes than by denying them even the most basic human sense of honor?

On the issues of honor, shame, and women's roles, Usama has so far proven to be quite conventional. Few men of his time would have quarreled with any of the values he airs in his writings. However, he is unique in that his love of noting unusual personal qualities often leads him to celebrate those few women who break the mold. If Burayka the witch represents all that is bad in a woman, others represent the highest places of virtue that women can attain. The piety of his grandmother has already been mentioned, as has his mother's willingness to sacrifice all to preserve her daughter's honor. The courage of his armor-clad aunt when Shayzar was invaded and the loyalty of his nurse Lu'lu'a have also been cited, and all proved cause for admiration from within his own household. But he didn't just praise women he knew. He also lauded the quick thinking of a woman when attacked by bandits (KI, 71–72 / 101), one who captured three Franks single-handed and even a woman who had her husband murdered because he was helping the Franks: "[w]e took into consideration what she did, and she remained with us treated with special regard and respect" (KI, 81–82 / 157–158). For Usama, these exceptional qualities allowed these women to rise, if only briefly, above average medieval Muslim women and the rules that bound them.

MALE HONOR AND SOCIAL STATUS

Other rules of conduct and status bound the lives of men. Subject to these rules himself, Usama was keenly aware of their importance and disturbed when they were transgressed. After all, he was himself the author of a manual on ideal (male) conduct, the *Kernels of Refinement*. Like many such manuals, it outlines all the qualities a man needs to possess true *adab*, the social graces of the day. But *adab* guides, like poetry, are heavily conventional, recycling tried and true poetic and prose selections to impress upon the reader the importance of tried and true social values. Far more revealing information about Usama's ideals of men's conduct comes from the subtle value judgments that he makes in his autobiographical anecdotes. Usama clearly encountered men he liked, and men whom he found wanting.

For Usama, men worthy of the name are honorable. They need not be wealthy nor of good family, although that helps quite a bit, as does being thin and handsome (as Usama modestly claims he was) and having a gift for interesting conversation and wit. Good penmanship was always an advantage, too. Real men are strong of body and constitution, like the lord of the castle of Abu al-Qubays who "could hold a horseshoe nail between his fingers and drive it into a board of oak wood" (KI, 118/148), or the soldier who, Usama reports, amputated his own diseased leg (KI, 146/175). They are serious-minded but not without being jovial; they respect their elders and superiors, and that includes God, even when they disagree; they reward acts of loyalty and service from their inferiors, never forgetting debts of any kind; they are generous in their hospitality, charitable to those in need, and never refuse an act of mercy when it is sought. Such men do not shun fighting or war if they are capable. They are brave, intrepid, and possessed of great resolution and perseverance. In battle they act as a team with their comrades, never abandoning them or failing to pitch in. "O what shame! By God, my death would truly be preferable to me than to flee!" exclaimed one Shayzari soldier, who later fled (KI, 62/91). Worthy men grow weary of the quiet life and refuse safe methods and easy answers. They are unflappable in stressful times and not easily confused or befuddled. Usama's model for unflappability is his father, who, surprised by a Frankish army while hunting, continued sucking on a quince he was enjoying while calmly escorting his boy out of harm's way (KI, 55/84). Good men may possess some or all of these qualities, but they should never, ever, succumb to pride, which always leads to doom.

Men like Usama were encouraged to acquire a strong sense of self-restraint, the classical Arab quality, *hilm* — he devotes a whole chapter to the subject in the *Kernels of Refinement*. Men who revealed their passions or beliefs too openly were considered weaklings; wearing one's heart on one's sleeve simply made it a better target. Hot-headedness was usually a trait of the young, and so older men were valued for their calm and experience. When Usama writes of "cooling down" the ranting young vizier of Egypt, he is fitting into an accepted social role (KI, 23/48). Dourness was frowned upon, and Usama subscribed to an emotional palette that would be recognized today as "Mediterranean." Machismo was the order of the day, although real men were allowed to cry, especially over honor or absent friends, who, when present, got kissed, hugged and fussed over (KI, 36/63) but morbid obsession, like that of a man from Shayzar whose daughter was captured by Franks, was a sign of madness, and too many tears wouldn't do (KI, 150/179). Public disputation was perfectly normal, but Usama considered it rude to wave one's hands about.

Any man that fell short in too many of these qualities was suspect, but Usama particularly disapproves of those who do not keep their oaths, are cowards, shirk their duty, or whine. Men who are easily bored or driven to amusement are also inadequate, and those who are greedy or disloyal are just plain bad.

Ideals of proper and improper behavior were especially important in the very male world of power and politics, where relationships were defined by formal ideas about friendship and patronage. Usama was a successful itinerant amir in Syria, Egypt, and northern Iraq not just because he was a good soldier, but also because he possessed the qualities of the male courtier, and so could serve a prince as counselor, companion, and surrogate brother, who posed no threat as a rival. Usama explicitly conceived of his bonds of service to his various patrons in terms of genealogy or friendship. He makes a point of saying how his former patrons sought him out after they lost him, and how he was their constant companion when they had his services, fighting, hunting, or relaxing at home. He even shared the same bed with the son of the vizier of Egypt whom he served, like a kinsman (KI, 20/45).

Bonds of formal friendship and rules of proper conduct were the markers that men of Usama's status deployed to maintain their standing, for separating the worthy from the unworthy, and for delimiting the hierarchy within those categories. Despite a prominent egalitarian strand in Islamic thought, the elite culture to which Usama subscribed was highly hierarchical. It is clear, even from a quick survey of his writings, that for Usama, social status was of far more consequence than religious or ethnic status. He was more likely to respect a Frankish knight than a Muslim peasant. Rank was one of the qualities that set truly civilized Muslims apart from the Franks, whose barbarity is clear from the fact that "they consider no precedence or high rank except that of the knights" (KI, 64/93). Such a simple way of bifurcating society (which is not an accurate description) must have seemed terribly crude to Usama, whose world was populated by all manner of men and women of many backgrounds and creeds who related to one another in different ways at different levels, signposting their relationships with unstated but perfectly clear marks of dress, conduct, and deportment. Once, Usama, in the midst of prayer in Jerusalem, was abruptly grabbed by a newly arrived Frank, who insisted he was praying in the "wrong" direction. For Usama, this was a great transgression of personal space and religious, social, and cultural boundaries. It must have seemed as if he had been attacked by a gorilla (KI, 134–135/163–164).

Hierarchy breeds competition, and Usama was very anxious to maintain his place in the pecking order. One of the clearest markers of social status was material wealth, and Usama reveals himself, in rather unflattering ways, to be borderline obsessive about his possessions. When the Byzantines pillaged Shayzar, Usama lamented his lost "tents, weapons, and furniture" in the same breath as his captured kinsmen and comrades (KI, 3/27). Usama has left barely any account of his time in the service of Unur of Damascus, but was careful to note that Unur "bestowed great gifts" on him, and that, obliged to flee to Egypt, he was forced to leave behind most of his belongings, which he called a "calamity" (KI, 4/28). Happily, everything turned out just fine in Egypt; the Fatimid caliph granted him the use of a posh house, "which was extremely magnificent, fully equipped with carpets, furniture, and a complete outfit of brass utensils" (KI, 6/30), and, he adds, he didn't have to give any of it back. Property was not merely a perquisite of his status: it *was* his status. When he needed to prove that a gilded saddle belonged to him, he knew it was inscribed with his name – but he had another irrefutable argument, for (KI, 9/55): "Who else [in those days] could ride in Egypt on a gold saddle but I?"

THE MANNERS AND CUSTOMS OF ANIMALS

In Usama's mind, qualities of distinction and rank were not a human monopoly. The animal world, too, had its ranks and divisions, its remarkable and despicable characters. Usama's world was, as has been noted, filled with animal life. In addition to the wild and domestic animals found in the caves, forests, rivers, deserts, fields, and homes of the medieval Middle East, there were the game animals that Usama and his kinsmen and companions hunted with such glee. Animals also provided amusement in races and in blood sports. When resting from the hunt, Usama's father enjoyed watching his dogs chase hares, for example. And hunting animals such as horses, dogs, or falcons that continually proved themselves became prized and even beloved additions to the household, even ransomed like captives if they fell into enemy hands.

The hunt was the principal activity that brought an aristocrat like Usama into contact with the animal world. As we have seen, hunting was a significant aspect of his life, especially in his younger days at Shayzar. Hunting provided him with a gentlemanly skill that increased his virtues as a princely companion for keen hunters like the atabeg Zangi. If hunting was important to Usama, it positively absorbed others. Chief among the most avid hunters was his father, Murshid. He was "always talking about it and about collecting birds of prey, considering no amount of expense too great for the satisfaction of his curiosity in this sport" (KI, 192/222). Such enthusiasm bred something akin to a hobbyist's network, as Murshid and his friends among the regional princes of the Near East exchanged hunting animals and corresponded to boast about their hunting exploits (KI, 225/254).

Usama's hunt-filled life afforded him ample opportunity to observe the ways of the bestial world, which, to him, oddly mirrored the human world. Horses and lions especially struck Usama as possessed of human traits. This was perfectly natural, as they were the most aristocratic of beasts. Arab authors wrote treatises on the genealogy of horses much as they did of the nobles of Arab tribes and:

"[t]here are among them, as among men, those which are enduring and others which are faint-hearted" (KI, 96/126). Usama described the perseverance of horses much as he did the extraordinary constitution of soldiers he had fought alongside and against, detailing their wounds and loyalty, and how they never weakened or quailed during times of violence and danger. He explicitly compares one horse with its rider, a Kurd, "a repository of valor," who, like his steed, kept fighting despite a gruesome lance thrust that pierced horse and horseman (KI, 95–96/126). Then there are horses of the other kind, such as the unhappy mount Usama rode once that, scratched by an arrow, fell to the ground in a fit (KI, 97–98/128).

As for lions, then as now, they were recognized as kings of beasts, feared by all animals. Lions were Usama's specialty, or so he boasted: "Indeed I have had more experience with lions and knowledge fighting them than any other person" (KI, 109/139). For all that, "I have seen lions do many things which I never expected them to do. Nor did I ever before believe that lions, like men, have among their number the courageous and the cowardly" (KI, 106/136). One lion killed and maimed most of Usama's hunting party, tearing through the hunters like a hurricane. But another lion, raised by a lion trainer in Damascus, drew only laughs. One day, the atabeg Unur asked that this lion be brought to the courtyard of his palace (KI, 106–107/137):

> Then he said to the master of his table, "Bring out a sheep from among the animals being prepared for slaughter for the kitchen and leave it in the inner court so that we may see how the lion annihilates it."... As soon as the sheep saw the lion, whose trainer had set it free from the chain which was around its neck, he rushed to it and butted it. The lion took to flight and began to circle around the pool with the sheep following behind, chasing and butting it. We were all overcome with laughter.

Unur considered this cowardly lion to be of ill-omen and ordered it killed and flayed. "As for the sheep," Usama adds, "it was exempted from ever being slaughtered."

Admirable qualities were not just limited to horses and lions; Usama noted when other beasts showed their mettle, such as a dog who valiantly protected his master from a lion attack (KI, 107/137), a leopard, known locally as "the holy-warrior leopard" who killed a Frankish knight (KI, 110–111/140), and a boar piglet, the size of a kitten, that had the pluck to butt at the hooves of the huntsmen's horses (KI, 224/252). Even geese, in Usama's judgment, had "fortitude and courage similar to the fortitude and courage of men" (KI, 217/245). It may be that such observations of human-like behavior were what allowed some people to sympathize with them, such as the tutor who calmly hid a partridge being pursued by his master's hunting-party, even telling the huntsmen that he hadn't seen it (KI, 215/244). Usama's father doted on prized hunting animals, including his falcon Yahshur, who was coddled and eventually given a ceremonial funeral in Hama (KI, 206/235–236), and a (relatively) docile cheetah that slept by his side (KI, 206–207/236).

But it would be a mistake to over-sentimentalize Usama's regard for animals. He was no environmentalist. For all that he admired the animal world, he conceived it as a realm for humans to dominate and bend to their will. In the end, the sheep-frightened lion was flayed, the plucky boar piglet was skewered on an arrow, and as for the partridge, its savior scholar tells us, the huntsmen "took it... broke its legs and threw it to the falcon, as my heart was breaking for it" (KI, 215/244). Where gazelles abounded in northern Iraq, the hundreds of young gazelles born the day or so before were seized while they slept "the same way that wood or grass is collected." This was not cruelty, but the law of the jungle, for "it is the nature of all animals for the strong to prey upon the weak" (KI, 226/254). In preying on the weakest of animals, in stalking the strongest and noblest lions, in recounting animal lore, their virtues and vices, raising and training other animals to hunt them, and killing, skinning, decapitating, and (sometimes) eating animals, Usama was exulting in his status as one of the "strong" and carefully distinguishing the world of real men from the world of weaker creatures, wise and wonderful, great and small.

CONCLUSION

Distinction is the one unifying thread throughout Usama's revealing statements about the way he conceived of his world, and how he saw it as a world of order pushing back a tide of chaos. Fate, God's will, religion, honor, manliness, and animals: if there is one theme that links these various preoccupations, it is order. Civilized humans are bound by rules – God's and ours – that guide our fate in this world and the next, and we must keep to them. Everything has its place in Usama's world, and its rank. Transgression of the rules and serious dissolution of social rank spelled chaos, leading to loss of status and, quite likely, hellfire. When the troops rebelled in Fatimid Cairo, opening a period of violence and madness that caused Usama to lose his carefully inventoried belongings, his patron, and his standing, and forced him to the ignominy of flight, Usama used the term *fitna* to describe the situation. This term describes not mere rebellion, but chaos and misrule of cosmic proportions.

Usama saw himself as a member of the most sublime group of people on earth – Muslim Arab men of noble birth – and was recognized as a particularly civilized member of this most civilized of groups. The stakes of keeping *fitna* locked up behind the social walls that penned it in were thus immense. Even as Usama strove earnestly to live an ordered life and maintain his status, there were others who might bring the whole works crashing down. Non-Muslims, people of low status, women, and even animals: these were parts of his world, but, in important ways, its very antithesis. Such potential sources of chaos needed to be regulated, if not subjugated. When, in his "memoirs," Usama writes about the non-Muslims, women, men, and animals that surpassed the standard rules of their station, one wonders whether he is celebrating these qualities so much as coming to terms with them by rendering potential sources of chaos merely as comforting and wondrous examples of the Almighty's unknowable decree.

FRANKS AND MUSLIMS

To his peers, Usama was first a poet and second an amir. Yet modern historians know Usama for his observations on the manners and customs of the Franks who inhabited parts of his world, perhaps the most famous of all the Arab eyewitnesses to the coming of the Franks to the medieval Near East. Usama's writings about the Franks are rich in ethnographic detail and dry wit, and so have been a favorite mine for information on Frankish–Muslim relations during the early phases of the Crusades. It is his anecdotes about the behavior of the Franks in Syria that keep Usama's writings in print and in textbooks, not his poetry. But, as I have tried to stress in the previous chapter, Usama's writings are deceptive in their "eyewitness" claims. To get a real sense of the value of Usama's observations on the Franks, one must have context, both for the kind of things that Muslims believed about Franks and for Usama's relations with Franks during his lifetime.

USAMA, ETHNOGRAPHER

Although Usama never refers to the Franks by anything other than the Arabic approximation *Ifranj*, the Europeans that he encountered were of diverse origins. The waves of conquest, pilgrimage, and settlement before the Third Crusade attracted men and women who were French, German, Norman, Lombard, Pisan, Venetian, Norwegian, Flemish, English, and more. Such diversity contributed to inter-Frankish rivalries in the Levant, and some writers of the age did take occasional account of such differences, noting the presence of English (*Intikar*), Germans (*Alman*), Venetians (*Banadiqa*) and so on. Usama seems not to have bothered with such distinctions, seeing the Franks as a more or less homogenous ethnic body. That most of his earliest experiences concerned Franks from the Norman-dominated Principality of Antioch may have contributed to this tendency to treat the Franks as a single ethnic group. This is clearest in Usama's occasional references to language. For Usama, all Franks (whatever their origins) speak a language called "Frankish" (*al-Ifranji*) which (along with Turkish) he admits he simply cannot understand (KI, 66/95). Yet, he inserts vocabulary of Frankish origin (as well as Turkish and Persian) in his text from time to time, most of it the untranslatable social vocabulary of his Frankish neighbors (*turkubuli*=turcopole; *sarjand*=serjeant; *burjasi*=burgess; *biskund*=viscount). "*Al-dama*," Usama elsewhere says in a knowing aside (KI, 136/165), "in their language means 'the lady'."

As is well known, the peoples of medieval Europe rather disappointed their Muslim observers in the Middle East. From an early date, the Franks left a reputation in the Islamic world as rough, unlettered barbarians famous, as Carole Hillenbrand has demonstrated, for their moral (especially sexual) laxity and their lack of cleanliness, stereotypes that collided with Muslim concerns over purity. Before the Crusades, when they spoke of Franks at all, it was in the realm of cosmography and descriptive geography, in which early Islamic scientists and travelers described distant corners of the known world and the *outré* customs of the odd peoples who lived there, as in this account by al-Mas'udi (cited in Hillenbrand, *Crusades*, 2000, 272):

> As regards the people of the northern quadrant, they are the ones for whom the sun is distant from the zenith ... such as the Slavs, the Franks, and those nations who neighbor them. The power of the sun is weak among them because of their distance from it; cold and damp prevail in their regions, and snow and ice follow one another in endless succession. The warm humor is lacking among them; their bodies are large, their natures gross, their manners harsh, their understanding dull, and their tongues heavy. Their color is so

excessively white that it passes from white to blue; their skin is thin and their flesh thick. Their eyes are also blue, matching the character of their coloring; their hair is lank and reddish because of the prevalence of damp mists. Their religious beliefs lack solidity …

Other geographers circulated similar tales of the inhabitants of the northern climes, noting their courage, their moral laxity, their casual attitude to personal hygiene, and their low intelligence. A tenth-century physician, Ibn al-Ash'ath, composed a *Book of Animals*, which featured a classification of human races. To him, the Franks, like other northerners, lack wisdom, and, like animals, they have only generic characteristics and lack all individuality. He also says they shed their hair annually, as do other beasts.

These are just a few of the ideas about the Franks that Usama inherited and, although he at least is able to rise slightly above them in matters of detail, most of the familiar ethnographic themes linger in his writings, foremost among them that of Frankish bestiality. For Usama, the Franks, though human, had oddly close affinities with the animal kingdom (KI, 132/161):

> Mysterious are the works of the Creator, the author of all things! When one comes to recount cases regarding the Franks … one sees them as animals possessing the virtues of courage and fighting, but nothing else; just as animals have only the virtues of strength and carrying loads.

The Franks are both possessed of animal qualities and devoid of civilized human traits. Like animals, they have neither jealousy nor zeal, but do have great courage (KI, 137/166). They are described as devils (KI, 134/163), dogs (KI, 91/121), and pigs (other writers continued the metaphor to other species and even to other phyla). The Franks that populate Usama's ecosystem have set ways, and like a naturalist, he made a practice of observing their ways, noting their habits and hangouts, just as he did with the lions, cheetahs, gazelles and geese that he hunted and like ducks and partridges, they congregate in specific places near Shayzar (KI, 43/71, 85/114). When killed in battle, Frankish heads were sometimes cut off and tallied or displayed by less polite warriors as trophies, precisely as was done with lions killed in the hunt (KI, 2/25; 149/178–179; 116/146).

If the Franks shared many qualities with animals, they fell short in some truly human qualities. As much as they can be lauded as warriors, they can be strangely timid (KA, 259/118):

> For I have battled the Franks — May God confound them! — in places and countries so numerous that I cannot count them, and I never once saw them defeat us and then persist in pursuing us, nor do their horses do more than amble or trot, fearing that some stratagem will befall them.

These strange and violent newcomers are said to have a "curious mentality," and to speak words "which would never come out of the head of a sensible man" (KI, 132/161). They are stupid, unlettered and do not control their women. They do not cover themselves in the bath, and they lack all sense of social order (KI, 74/93): "The Franks ... possess none of the virtues of men except courage, consider no precedence or high rank except that of knights, and have nobody that counts except knights." Though, on this subject, Usama does suggest that knightliness is culturally relative (KI, 75/94):

> The [Frankish] king said to me..., "I was told that you were a great knight, but I did not believe previous to that that you were really a knight." "O my lord," I replied, "I am a knight according to the manner of my race and my people." If the knight is thin and tall the Franks admire him more.

Knights, kings, or commoners, Franks for Usama are paradigmatic barbarians, innocent of the capability to speak any noble tongue. As Usama complained (with evident exaggeration) of the futility of cross-cultural encounters, "These people speak nothing but Frankish; we do not understand what they say" (KI, 66/95). Finally, they are an accursed race and do not assimilate except with members of their own kin (KI, 130/159), although, as we shall see, it's the newcomers you have to watch out for; once the Franks get acclimated to the Middle East, some of them can be quite good chaps (KI, 134/163).

Despite his personal acquaintance with Frankish culture and individual Franks, it turns out that Usama does not really contribute much more than the stock stereotypes about the Franks of his day; his perception of the Franks was even more monolithic than that of other (albeit later) Muslim observers. It follows that as a source for Frankish life in the medieval Levant, his contribution should not be exaggerated.

As with any single source, Usama's writings are more valuable for certain aspects of Frankish–Muslim relations than for others. On economic relationships in the medieval Levant, he has virtually nothing to say, except in so far as such relationships intersect with his other interests, such as his story about the trade in hunting birds and dogs across the Byzantine frontier (KI, 199/228). Usama is most valuable for what he tells us about two aspects of Frankish–Muslim relations: local politics and social relations. However, even in these areas, his contributions come with qualifications. Despite the rich detail they sometimes offer, Usama's writings are not, to be perfectly honest, very good sources for the history of Frankish–Muslim political relations. With the exception of an anecdote here or there, Usama does not relate detailed narratives of battles with the Franks of the sort one finds in medieval chronicles, nor does he provide much of a portrait of any of the principal personages he writes about, such as one might find in biographical dictionaries. What he does provide, however, is a localized and personal view of some of the events, people and practices of the period, which fills some of the gaps in our knowledge of this complicated history, particularly with reference to affairs in northern Syria.

USAMA AND THE COMING OF THE CRUSADES

Usama was born in 1095, the year in which Pope Urban II called for what would turn out to be the First Crusade, so he was too young to have any memory of the progress of that crusade through Syria toward Jerusalem, although, in 1098, Shayzar did play a role in its course. The Franks had already ravaged the surrounding countryside and captured heavily fortified towns and cities in the region amidst rumors of dire ferocity. Rather than attempt to fight this menace,

Usama's uncle, Sultan, sought a different path. As the Franks, under Raymond of Toulouse, set out toward Shayzar from nearby Ma'arrat al-Nu'man, a Frankish chronicler tells us (Peter Tudebode, *Historia*, 1977, 128/104):

> The king of Shayzar ... sent his couriers to Raymond ... both while he was at Ma'arrat al-Nu'man and in Kafartab. They carried word that their king wished to accord with Raymond and to give as much from his revenue as the count demanded. Further, the emissaries said the king of Shayzar desired to be diligent in helping the Christians, and he pledged to make pilgrims secure and free of fear so far as his jurisdiction permitted. He also offered to furnish a market in horses and food. As a result the pilgrims moved out and pitched their tents along the Orontes near Shayzar.

Sultan also provided the Crusaders with guides, who led them west across the Orontes and safely through his own territory.

The sequel is of course well known: the Franks captured Jerusalem in July of 1099 and, by July of 1109, had established four Frankish holdings in the region: the County of Edessa, the Principality of Antioch, the Latin Kingdom of Jerusalem, and the County of Tripoli. As with most events that occurred outside the orbit of Shayzar, Usama has almost nothing to say about the coming of the Franks (perhaps because of his uncle's pragmatic conciliatory attitude), save one, almost passing, comment introducing a longer tale (LA, 132):

> When the Franks – may God confound them – came in the year 1096 and conquered Antioch and were victorious over the armies of Syria, they were seized with greed and gave themselves up to fancies of possessing Baghdad and the lands of the East.

Usama's recollection of the First Crusade is interesting in that it differs from the interpretations to be found in other medieval observers of the Franks (Hillenbrand, *Crusades*, 2000, 50–54), which generally seem to have quite a good sense of what it was about. For example, one chronicler of Aleppo, al-'Azimi (writing in about 1160) saw the First Crusade as revenge for alleged Muslim mistreatment of Frankish pilgrims, a view shared by Pope Urban II in some versions of his sermon at Clermont (see Peters, *First Crusade*,1998, 25–37). One contemporary statement (in about 1105), by a Muslim preacher of Damascus, al-Sulami, explicitly refers to the Crusades as a *jihad* or holy war, and blames Muslim losses on the selfish ambitions of their backsliding leaders. Others saw the First Crusade as part of a larger pattern of Christian expansion into the margins of the Islamic world: Spain, Sicily, North Africa, and now Syria, a view compatible with those of al-'Azimi or al-Sulami. Ibn al-Athir (died 1233), a later historian, specifically mentions Jerusalem as the Crusader goal, and, like al-Sulami, calls the Frankish assault a *jihad* (but this is no doubt the result of hindsight). Then again, Ibn al-Athir also suggested that the Fatimids had invited the Franks to invade Syria, and that their alliance lay behind Frankish successes, a clear Sunni attempt to blame the Shi'ite Fatimids. Usama is silent on the matter of the Crusade's original aim, but his assertion that the Franks desired to conquer Baghdad once they arrived appears to be unique. The account is of further note because it was written in 1183, over eighty years after the coming of the Franks. Even at that date, someone who was as interested in history and as well acquainted with the Franks as Usama still had only a vague sense of the goals of the First Crusade, despite the fair degree of accuracy on the part of other Muslim observers. Of course, it's possible that Usama knew more about the Crusades than he tells us.

USAMA ON ANTIOCH

With the four Frankish states established, geopolitical realties dictated the incidence of Frankish military pressure on Muslim lands. Shayzar's main Frankish enemy was the Principality of Antioch in the north, not the Kingdom of Jerusalem in the south. Frankish Antioch's desire to dislodge Usama's family from Shayzar forms the context for the various battles in northern Syria in general, and around Shayzar in particular, that Usama mentions in his accounts of his younger days.

The Principality of Antioch had a rocky start. In 1103, five years after the Franks conquered the city, the combined forces of Antioch and Edessa were defeated in battle on the Khabur River in northern Iraq by the Saljuq governor of Mosul. Baldwin and Joscelin of Edessa were captured and remained in Muslim hands until 1108. In the interim, Frankish leaders had begun to contend with one another. By late 1108, relations between Antioch and Edessa had broken down to the extent that Tancred, lord of Antioch, and Ridwan, the Muslim lord of Aleppo, united against Baldwin and Joscelin, who, in their turn, formed an alliance with their Muslim former captor against Tancred and Ridwan. The result was one of those messy Frankish–Muslim alliances that would have scandalized the more fervent participants in the First Crusade. It also resulted in a massive battle, during which, Usama recounted, "the blows of the swords between [the rival Frankish armies] were like the blows of axes on cordwood" (LA, 134). Tancred and Ridwan were victorious.

Tancred ruled Antioch until his death in 1112. He was not, Usama warns us, a man to be trusted. After a temporary truce had been declared between Shayzar and Antioch, Usama's uncle sent a prized horse as tribute to Tancred. The horse was led by a young Kurdish horseman, Hasanun, who raced against some of the Frankish horsemen in Tancred's camp and out-paced them all. As a reward, Tancred bestowed robes of honor on Hasanun, but he wanted only Tancred's guarantee of safety should he fall into Frankish hands in time of war. This Tancred granted, but, a year later, after the truce had lapsed, Hasanun was taken captive and "the Franks inflicted all kinds of torture on him." His captors had wanted to put out his left eye (KI, 66/95):

> But Tancred (may God's curse be upon him!) said to them, "Rather put out his right eye, so that when he carries his shield his left eye will be covered, and he will be no more able to see anything." So they put out his right eye in accordance with Tancred's orders and demanded as a ransom from him one thousand dinars and a black horse ... one of the most magnificent horses. My father ransomed him with that horse.

Ultimately, the Banu Munqidh were defeated and Tancred imposed a heavy tribute on Shayzar, which remained in place well after his death.

Roger of Salerno (1112–1119) succeeded Tancred. Though Usama refers to him as "a devil of the Franks" (KI, 118/148), he kept on relatively good terms with Shayzar, which was, after all, in a tributary relationship with Antioch, paying annual sums of cash and occasional service, as when Roger, probably around 1116, demanded that the Banu Munqidh provide an escort for one his messengers bound for Jerusalem. Usama particularly remembered the compliment that the messenger paid to his uncle Sultan's statecraft (KI, 87/117):

> When the knight met my uncle he said, "My lord has dispatched me on business and a secret mission. But seeing that you are an intelligent man, I will disclose it to you." My uncle said, "How do you know that I am an intelligent man, when you have never seen me before this moment?" The knight replied, "Because I noticed that the whole region I passed through was in ruins except for your domains, which are flourishing."

Usama's impression of Roger as a devilish threat to the Muslims is probably due to Roger's stunning success in the field against Bursuq, the Saljuq atabeg of Mosul, at the battle of Danith in 1115. Usama's father was among the Muslim troops who were forced into humiliating retreat that day (KI, 85–86/105):

> By the decree of God … our army departed from Kafartab to Danith and were surprised to meet … the army of Antioch [under Roger]. The Amir al-Sayyid [one of Bursuq's commanders] was killed, together with a large body of Muslims … We then left Kafartab and returned to Shayzar in the company of my father, who had lost all the tents, loads, mules, camels and baggage he had, and whose army was dispersed.

Roger eventually got his comeuppance. In 1119, in one of the most devastating losses of the early Crusades, the army of Antioch was almost wiped out, as it stood surrounded by the forces of Ilghazi, lord of Aleppo. So heavy was the defeat that the locality became known as *ager sanguinis*: the Field of Blood. Usama noted, with hyperbolic relish, that Ilghazi "killed [Roger] and slaughtered his entire army, of which less than twenty men returned to Antioch" (KI, 119/148).

At Roger's death, King Baldwin II of Jerusalem was obliged to step in as regent of Antioch until the young prince Bohemond II's arrival in 1126. Though this period was one of warmer connections between Shayzar and Antioch, Usama claims that Baldwin was only able to reach Antioch because Ilghazi had given himself up to drink in the wake of his victory at the Field of Blood. That said, Usama clearly has a positive view of Baldwin. Having been a guest of the Banu Munqidh at Shayzar while his release from captivity was being negotiated, Baldwin gave them special treatment, freeing them of the odious obligation of tribute laid upon them since the time of Tancred and, if Usama is to be believed, allowing them to have a certain amount of influence in the affairs of Antioch (KI, 121/150).

Usama is less sanguine about Bohemond II, Baldwin's successor in Antioch, son and heir of Antioch's first lord, Bohemond of Taranto. In 1126, the young man finally arrived in the Levant to claim his inheritance. Usama preserves an account of the banalities of the transition to power (KI, 121/150):

> As Baldwin was occupying his position as king [in Antioch] and while he was receiving an envoy of ours, there arrived ... a ship carrying a lad in rags. This lad presented himself before Baldwin and introduced himself to him as the son of Bohemond. Baldwin thereupon delivered Antioch to him, left it and pitched his tents outside of the city. Our envoy ... stated to us on his oath that he, King Baldwin, bought the fodder for his horses that night from the market, while the granaries of Antioch were overflowing with provender. Baldwin then returned to Jerusalem.

Usama here casts Baldwin as endowed with the humble dignity that was considered an ideal trait in Muslim rulers, as seen in the pious caliph 'Umar or, more to the point, in Nur al-Din and Saladin. Bohemond II, the eighteen-year-old "lad in rags," by contrast, is guilty of that most ignoble of Arab sins: poor hospitality. Worse still, "that devil, the son of Bohemond, proved a terrible calamity to our people." Indeed, it was only his cowardice that saved him from death at the hands of the troops of Shayzar, if not those of Usama himself, during one skirmish (KI, 121–122/151):

> Among our troops was a Kurd named Mikha'il, who now came fleeing before the van of their infantry, followed by a Frankish knight and hard pressed by him. The Kurd was screaming before the Frank and howling aloud ... I kept behind him and spurred my horse forward to overtake him, so that I might give him a blow with the lance, but my horse could not overtake him ... My comrades then dealt a lance blow to his horse which all but finished it. Soon his comrades were coming to his assistance in such great number that we should be powerless before them. The Frankish knight now turned back, with his horse gasping its last, met his comrades and ordered them all to retire ... This knight was none other than the son of Bohemond, lord of Antioch, who, being still a lad, had his heart filled with fright. Had he let his comrades come, they would have defeated us and chased us back to town.

In time, Bohemond II, too, met his fate, killed in 1130 fighting a Turkish dynasty in Cilicia; his head was sent to the caliph in Baghdad.

Usama left no reaction to this news. In the following year, he was packing his things and exiled from Shayzar. By 1138, he was in service to the Muslim lord of Damascus, involved in diplomatic relations with the Kingdom of Jerusalem, which marked an important change in his relations with the Franks. By then, the first generation of Franks in the Near East had effectively died out. All the leaders associated with the First Crusade and its aftermath – the Baldwins and the Bohemonds, Raymond, Tancred and Joscelin – had passed on. The political fortunes of the Frankish states were in the hands of a younger generation, many born in the Levant, for whom frontier living was a normal way of life and for whom Crusading zeal had given way to accommodation. And, while he would still engage the Franks in battle and on diplomatic missions, Usama would never again encounter them as frequently as he did at Shayzar, in the very marches of Antioch. After Usama fled Damascus for Fatimid Cairo, even the Second Crusade passed by as distant news, and he reports it merely as the setting for the exemplary tale of the Damascene ascetic hero al-Findalawi, who died in the fighting (KI, 95/124). As Usama busied himself in his ambitious life, making the circuit of the major courts of the medieval Middle East, the Frankish invaders settled in as one of many political entities on the Levantine landscape.

SOCIAL RELATIONS WITH THE FRANKS

The fact that the Franks were beginning to blend into Levantine culture and society was not lost on contemporary observers. In a famous passage, the Frankish chronicler Fulcher of Chartres (died about 1127) urges his readers, much as Usama likes to do, to use the case of the Franks to reflect on God's inscrutable plan (Fulcher, *Historia*, 1913, III.xxxvii/271–272):

> I pray you, consider and reflect on how God has in our times changed West into East. For we, who were occidentals, have now become orientals. The man who was a Roman or a Frank has, in this land, been turned into a Galilean or a Palestinian. He who was once a citizen of Reims or of Chartres has now become a citizen of Tyre or Antioch ... One among us now has his own houses and retainers, just as if he possessed them through hereditary or family right. Another takes as his wife, not a woman of his own stock, but rather a Syrian or Armenian, or even, occasionally, a Saracen who has obtained the grace of baptism ... Men address one another in turn in the speech and idiom of various languages.

Usama, too, was aware of these cultural changes. "Among the Franks," he writes in his *Book of Learning* (KI, 140/169–170), "are those who have become acclimatized and have associated long with the Muslims. These are much better than the recent arrivals from the Frankish lands. But they constitute the exception and cannot be treated as a rule." As an example, Usama relates an episode told to him by one of his men who had been invited to the home of a retired Frankish knight in Antioch:

> We came to the home of a knight who belonged to the old category of knights who came with the early expeditions of the Franks. He had been by that time stricken off the register and exempted

from service, and possessed in Antioch an estate on the income of which he lived. The knight presented an excellent table, with food extraordinarily clean and delicious. Seeing me abstaining from food, he said, "Eat, be of good cheer! I never eat Frankish dishes, but have Egyptian woman cooks and never eat except their cooking. Besides, pork never enters my home."

Elsewhere, Usama points out the differences between Franks who were long-time residents of the Levant and the rough newcomers, a distinction noted in other Arab authors of the era, who often speak of "western Franks" fresh from Europe and the settled "coastal" or "Syrian Franks" (KI, 134/163): "Everyone who is a fresh emigrant from the Frankish lands is ruder in character than those who have become acclimatized and have held long association with the Muslims." His example is a new arrival who, seeing Usama praying (with the permission of friends among the Templars) in the al-Aqsa mosque in Jerusalem, grabbed him and turned him to the East, saying "This is the way you should pray!" Usama's comments on the events that followed indicate his disdain for such newcomers (KI, 134–35/164):

The Templars came in to him and expelled him. They apologized to me, saying, "This is a stranger who has only recently arrived from the land of the Franks and he has never before seen anyone praying except eastward." Thereupon I said to myself, "I have had enough of prayer." So I went out and have ever since been surprised at the conduct of this devil of a man, at the change in the color of his face, his trembling and his sentiment at the sight of one praying [south, towards Mecca].

As noted earlier, Usama had come to Jerusalem sometime in the period 1138–1144 during his tenure at the court of the Burid ruler of Damascus, and the voyages he made there with the amir Unur serve as the basis for much of what he reports about social relations between Franks and Muslims. In previous chapters, I have already made reference to some of the kinds of Frankish–Muslim social relations of which Usama was aware: warfare, certainly, but also ransoming, diplomacy, commerce, feasting, and even bathing.

These stories testify to the complexity of Usama's own individual relationships with Franks. Franks were, of course, outsiders and opponents in war; at times, however, they might also be friends. Muslims engaged in non-military missions could mix readily with them, such as the servant of Usama's who dined in Antioch. In Jerusalem, Usama himself was engaged in diplomatic work, and this surely encouraged at least a veneer of amicability, such as the members of the Templars in Jerusalem whom Usama names as friends (KI, 134/163–164), or the household of the Frankish baron William of Bures, who feted Usama and Unur in Tiberias (KI, 137/167). The fact that Franks and Muslims of Usama's status shared a similar code of chivalrous male conduct undoubtedly assisted their sociability. The shared values of the Frankish and Muslim elite explain how Usama could befriend not just a Frankish knight, but a new arrival – precisely the sort of Frank he warned his readers about. Of this man, Usama says (KI, 132/161) that he "was of my intimate fellowship and kept such constant company with me that he began to call me 'my brother'. Between us there were mutual bonds of amity and friendship." However, the relationship was not strictly fraternal, as Usama goes on to mock the knight for offering to take his son Murhaf back to Europe to be educated, a bullet of inter-cultural hospitality he only narrowly dodged (KI, 132/161). What he did not realize was that he was ridiculing an invitation that indicated great esteem among the Franks, as a later Syrian Christian knew very well (Barhebraeus, *Butyrum sapientiae*, 2004, 2.2.8):

> In our times [the 13th century], the princes of the Franks have the very same custom [as the ancient Persians]. They let their children enter the service of their allies, so that they will be educated amidst the servants of the latter, and learn discipline and humility together with them and in like manner. Accordingly, they shall deserve the honor of their fathers.

It was a lost opportunity. For Usama, it was perfectly acceptable to appreciate Franks of a certain standing; but one did not want to overdo it. The same could be said of his attitude toward three areas of Frankish–Muslim interaction that particularly drew his attention: medicine, law, and religion.

MEDICINE

The field of medicine was certainly one in which Franks and Muslims met with great frequency, and in which Usama was greatly interested. In his world, physicians, whether of Christian, Jewish, or Muslim origin, served Frankish and Muslim patients alike, crossing territorial, religious and social borders with regularity. A famous example is Ya'qub ibn Siqlab, a Christian from Frankish Jerusalem who studied and practiced in that city before becoming a court physician in Damascus under one of Saladin's successors. It was a Christian physician of Shayzar who recounted to Usama one of the most famous anecdotes in his *Book of Learning*. A Frankish lord had asked Usama's uncle to send him this physician to tend to two Frankish patients (KI, 132–333/162):

> They brought before me a knight in whose leg an abscess had grown, and a woman afflicted with imbecility. To the knight I applied a small poultice ... and the woman I put on a special diet [to balance her humors]. Then a Frankish physician came to them and said: "This man knows nothing about treating them." He then said to the knight: "Which would you prefer, living with one leg or dying with two?" The latter replied: "Living with one leg." The physician said: "Bring me a strong knight and a sharp axe." So a knight came with the axe, [and so this strong knight] struck [the patient's leg] with one blow while I was looking on, but the leg was not severed. So he dealt another blow, upon which the marrow of the leg flowed out and the patient died on the spot. He then examined the woman and said: "This is a woman in whose head there is a demon that has possessed her. Shave off her hair." So they shaved it off and the woman began once more to eat their diet – garlic and mustard. Her imbecility took a turn for the worse, so the physician said: "The demon has penetrated through her head." He therefore took a razor, made a deep cruciform incision on [her head], peeled back the skin ... and rubbed it with salt. The woman also expired instantly. Thereupon I asked them whether my services were needed any longer, and when they replied in the negative I returned home, having learned of their medicine what I previously knew not.

This story could be the most frequently cited anecdote in Usama's *Book of Learning*, and is often used as the *sole* piece of evidence that Islamic medicine (or even Islamic culture in general) was greatly in advance of the Franks'. However, there are three principal flaws in that line of thought. First, many of Usama's anecdotes should be taken with a grain of salt, not least when they are about Franks: one would hardly take his stories about Frankish women completely at face value, for example. Second, his story tells us less about reality than about perceptions. In reality, Frankish medicine was not, on the whole, radically less sophisticated than that practiced by the physicians of the Islamic world, as we know from other evidence. True, Usama is clearly horrified by the "medicine" in this tale, as he is by a priest who euthanizes, rather than heals, an ailing knight (KI, 137–138/166–167). But the practices he claims to be so horrified by could be found in Islamic medicine too: both Frankish and Islamic systems of medicine were pluralistic, involving both what we might now call "scientific" approaches to healing and "folkloric" practices (prayers, amulets, and the like). And, if good physicians in Usama's world did not exactly jump at the opportunity to amputate, the practice was hardly unknown. Nor were other practices that even the Franks would have found brutal. While it is true that Islamic medicine could boast a relatively untroubled familiarity with the medical lore of antiquity (such as that of Galen), medieval Europeans were catching up in this regard on the eve of the Crusades. On the whole, patients probably faced no better or worse chance of recovery under either system. What Usama found troubling about Frankish medicine was less the practices involved than the character of the physician, whom Usama saw as a rough and impatient healer who chose the most drastic remedy without a moment's deliberation.

Usama's accounts of Frankish (and Islamic) medicine are thus better seen as evidence of contemporary perceptions and attitudes. It must be said that many of his contemporaries, even some Frankish writers, *perceived* Islamic medicine to be somehow superior to that of the Franks. A famous Frankish account of an alleged attempt by a Syrian physician to poison King Baldwin III attests to resentment of the fact that Christian rulers preferred eastern doctors over their

Latin counterparts (William of Tyre, *Chronicon*, 1986, xviii.34/ II:292–93):

> Our eastern princes, through the influence of their women, scorn the medicines and practice of our Latin physicians and believe only in Jews, Samaritans, Syrians, and Saracens. Most recklessly they put themselves under the care of such practitioners and trust their lives to people who are ignorant of the science of medicine.

The third flaw in relying too heavily upon Usama's long anecdote is that it does not represent the full spectrum of his representations of either Islamic or Frankish medicine: he is not unrelentingly negative about Frankish medicine. Just after the anecdote lampooning the Frankish physician and his "treatment" of his two patients, Usama narrates a successful example of Frankish medicine that he had witnessed himself (KI, 133–134/162–163):

> The king of the Franks had for treasurer a knight named Bernard who (May God curse him!) was one of the most accursed and wicked of the Franks. A horse kicked him in the leg, which was subsequently infected and which opened in fourteen different places. Every time one of those cuts would close in one place, another would open in another place. All this happened while I was praying for his perdition. Then came to him a Frankish physician and removed from the leg all the ointments which were on it and began to wash it with very strong vinegar. By this treatment all the cuts were healed and the man became well again. He was up again like a devil.

Usama also describes a Frankish treatment of scrofula that was so successful that he used it himself. Thus, if we admit that his perception of Frankish medicine was a broadly negative one (which was in line with the prejudices of his day), we must also admit that it was not unremittingly so.

FRANKISH JUSTICE

The same cannot be said about the realms of law and religion, in both of which Usama saw unambiguous examples of Frankish failings.

During his travels in their territory, Usama witnessed Frankish justice on numerous occasions and in one instance, he was personally
involved. Some flocks belonging to his Muslim neighbors had strayed
into the forests around the Frankish border town of Baniyas and had
been captured by the lord's knights, in contravention of the truce.
Usama won his suit and the lord of Baniyas was obliged to pay a fine.
But what startled Usama was the high legal authority that knights
– mere warriors, after all – held, for the men who deliberated and
settled the affair were not men trained in law, nor members of the
learned classes (the 'ulama'), as would be the case in an Islamic setting, but knights, men noted for their courage, but not necessarily
discernment or familiarity with the divine order. "Such a judgment,"
Usama explains, "after having been pronounced by the knights, not
even the king nor any of the chieftains of the Franks can alter or
revoke" (KI, 39–40/93–94).

In Nablus, he was even less impressed, not to say horrified, by
Frankish justice in the form of a duel (KI, 84–85/167–168). A
Frankish peasant was charged with having assisted Muslim bandits in
their attack on a local village: he responded by petitioning the king,
Fulk of Anjou, and challenged his accuser to a duel. The peasant, an
old man, had little chance against his opponent, the village smith, so
he lost his case, and also his life: "They then fastened a rope around
the neck of [the dead peasant], dragged him away and hanged him
... This case illustrates the kind of jurisprudence and legal decisions
the Franks have – may God's curse be upon them!"

On another journey through Nablus, Unur and Usama encountered a blind Muslim whose polite manner caught their attention
(139/168):

> I inquired about this man and was informed that his mother had been
> married to a Frank whom she had killed. Her son used to practice
> ruses against the Frankish pilgrims and co-operate with his mother
> in killing them. They finally brought charges against him and tried his
> case according to the Frankish way of procedure.

The "Frankish way of procedure" was trial by water: if, dunked into a
cask of water, the man sank, he was considered innocent and pulled

to safety. But if he floated, he was guilty: "The man did his best to sink when they dropped him in the water, but he could not do it. So he had to submit to their sentence against him – may God's curse be upon them!" He was blinded with red-hot awls. He later entered the service of Unur in Damascus and was given a stipend from the treasury. Interestingly, Usama is upset by the verdict imposed despite the fact that the man was, by his own account, guilty.

What shocked Usama about these manifestations of Frankish justice was not only the brutality of the punishments involved (medieval Islamic law had its share of gruesome penalties, as Usama was no doubt aware), but the illogical and indeed godless basis for their dispensation. This is hardly fair: while the ordeal was provided for in the Crusader states at an early stage (as decreed by a synod of Nablus), one needs only to look at the later compendium of Frankish law, the *Assizes of Jerusalem*, to realize that formal Frankish law was a thorough and fairly complicated affair. For Usama, what mattered was the public manifestation of the law, since this was all that he ever saw. When he mocks the duel in Nablus as an example of Frankish "jurisprudence and legal decisions," he is using technical terms from the field of Islamic law to show how different he sees the two systems to be. Jurisprudence, or *fiqh,* is a delicate field of scholarship, requiring highly skilled religious scholars, proofs in sacred law, and a patient application of reason (when advisable). For Usama, nothing could be further from the intricacies of applying sacred law, the *shari'a*, than the sight of this wiry peasant being publicly cudgeled to death by the village blacksmith, or the Muslim highwayman desperately trying to sink to the bottom of the cask in a last futile attempt to put one over on the Franks.

USAMA AND CHRISTIANITY

As with his reflections on Frankish concepts of justice, Usama leaves little room for the merits of Latin Christianity. Muslims were, of course, acquainted with Middle Eastern Christians and Christianity from the very beginning. The Qur'an itself has much to say about

Christianity and its followers, but its evaluation of Christianity is mixed: appreciation for the figures of Jesus and Mary and the place of Christianity in the history of God's covenant with humanity is combined with denunciation of what was seen as Christianity's poly-theistic trinitarianism. In the centuries between the Qur'an and Usama, Muslim lawyers, theologians, and polemicists had developed these themes, showing detailed familiarity with Christian scripture, theology and religious practice. Of course, none of these writers ever stopped feeling frustrated by the fact that a community like the Christians, "People of the Book," could dwell in full witness of the victory of Islam and its teachings and still refuse to embrace it. Then again, much the same story of tension and distrust could be told of medieval Christian reactions to Islam. Inter-faith understanding is a concern of our world, not Usama's.

Nevertheless, Usama had no real trouble with Christianity. Shay-zar was, probably, a largely Christian town when Usama lived there; the subjects of his family certainly were (recall the Easter festivities that the men of the household were attending when their castle was besieged by Nizaris). Christian servants, physicians, merchants, and workmen were all around him in his youth. Beyond Shayzar, his knowledge of the Christian world of the Middle East broad-ened. He admired the personal piety and convictions of a Coptic patriarch he encountered in Egypt, and was moved – not to say troubled – by the exertions of the monks in the church of St. John at Sebaste. But Christian concepts of God offended his sensibilities (KI, 135/164):

> I saw one of the Franks come to [the amir Unur] when he was in the Dome of the Rock [which the Franks had converted into a church] and say to him, "Do you want to see what God looked like as a child?" [Unur] said, "Yes." The Frank walked ahead of us until he showed us the picture of Mary with Jesus (may peace be upon him!) as an infant in her lap. He then said, "This is God as a child." But God is exalted far above what the infidels say about him!

Usama was of the belief that the Franks were constitutionally inca-pable of relinquishing their habits (with a few exceptions), and this extended into their religion. Usama was wary of Frankish converts, for, as much as the process of conversion might seem to be a victory for Islam, it never seemed to "take." He recalls a Frankish woman and her son who had been captured at Shayzar (KI, 130–131/160):

> The son accepted Islam, and his conversion was genuine, judging by what he showed in the practice of prayer and fasting. He learned the art of working marble from a stonecutter who had paved the home of my father. After staying for a long time with us my father gave him as wife a woman who belonged to a pious [Muslim] family, and paid all necessary expenses for his wedding and home. His wife bore him two sons. The boys grew up. When they were five or six years old, their father, young Ra'ul, who was very happy at having them, took them with their mother and everything that his house contained and on the second morning joined the Franks in Apamea, where he and his children became Christians, after having practiced Islam with its prayers and faith. May God therefore purify the world from such people!

Despite the real military threat posed by the Franks to Usama at Shayzar and elsewhere during his long life, it is clear from his writings that what most troubled him about the Franks, as it did many other Muslims, was that they posed a special double threat. In Usama's day, warlike barbarians with odd customs were no great thing: he need only think of the Berbers of North Africa centuries ago and the Turks more recently. Nor was Christianity much of a worry. Muslims of Usama's day thought the failings of Christian theology to be self-evident, and took the fact that Islam had defeated the Christian world in the past to presage its ultimate submission. But the Berbers and Turks had seen the light and the native Christians of Usama's world were subjects who knew their place. Neither was true of the Franks. Infidels *and* aliens, the Franks would neither submit to God's will nor accept protection as subordinates of His earthly followers. Managing encounters with such a threat required sticking to one's cultural guns and asserting one's spiritual and civilizational superiority, for example by telling witty yarns and ribald tales. Have you heard the one about the knight and the Frankish doctor?

As a source for information about daily life in the Frankish Levant, Usama has his limitations; as an example of Muslim attitudes to Frankish culture, he is far more valuable. A cultivated Muslim, he could be stunned and amused by the curious customs of these out-landers, even admire some of them; yet at the same time, he could (and probably should) fight them, revile them and, like so many other Muslim writers of the day, wish God to curse them, confound them, and, quite explicitly, *not* let His mercy rest upon their souls.

AFTERWORD

PEER: When will the core emerge into light?
[Pulls the whole onion to pieces.]
God knows if it will. Right down to the centre
It's nothing but layers, getting smaller and smaller.
Nature's a joker!
[He casts away the rest.]

Henrik Ibsen, Peer Gynt, Act 5, Scene v

W as Usama ibn Munqidh really a "Maker of the Muslim World," as the title of this book series suggests? The many layers that intervene between a contemporary observer and the historical Usama make a quick answer difficult. Indeed, the question raises a further conundrum: just who was the real Usama? Once we peel away the evaluations and commentary of modern biographers and historians, we are confronted with Usama's medieval biographers: peel away their representations, and we are left with Usama's depiction of himself. We can go no further toward the "real" Usama than that. There is, nevertheless, a great consensus among these sources, and if consensus doesn't really wash as "fact," lacking any better evidence, it will have to do for now.

Usama's life was one of great activity, played out on a grand political stage populated by Frankish lords and ladies, and Muslim princes, generals, and sultans. His exploits in battle made him prized by his patrons and famed among his contemporaries. His medieval biographers called him a hero (*batal*), a paladin (*faris*), an amir, son of amirs, possessing the manly qualities of grace and leadership expected of someone of such stature. For Hartwig Derenbourg, the French Orientalist who wrote the first modern biography over a century ago, Usama had the makings of a classic Romantic hero, complete with troubled (yet noble) upbringing. Derenbourg describes Usama's formative years with his father at Shayzar thus (Derenbourg, *Vie*, 1889, 41):

> As for the soul of the young Usama, it leapt into action from the sting of reproof. These circumstances created a hero, full of deference and admiration for [his father], but determined to imitate him as more the warrior than the ascetic, the adversary of the Franks more than the calligrapher, the man of resolute action more than the mystic absorbed in the recitation and copying of the Qur'an.

Derenbourg and his subject are here in complete agreement, for this was certainly the side of his personality that Usama, no stranger to vanity, tried to stress in his *Book of Learning by Example*.

But, to be accurate, Usama never played more than a supporting role in the political morality plays of his day, one in which he appears less as a maker of anything than as its exploiter. For his patrons he filled a specific niche as a warrior and, one could also say, as a status symbol. Usama added luster to the courts of rough-hewn Saljuq warlords like Zangi, an Arabic high cultural sheen that they would otherwise lack. That he also provided them with local connections and intelligence would have been icing on the cake. In such roles, Usama was not really actively forging the destiny of the states he served: indeed, one could argue that his inept attempts at palace intrigue in Cairo and elsewhere may actually have contributed to the weakness of the courts he was supposed to be defending. His one constant but unspoken ambition – to return to Shayzar and rule – was never realized, and he remained thwarted and frustrated in his attempts to carve out his own realm. Instead, throughout his life, he survived by working for others, a restless dependent of patronage, not a source of it himself.

Usama's relatively humble place on the political stage did not seem to bother his contemporaries, for they cherished his literary achievements above all his other accomplishments. For Usama's peers and for later generations of medieval Muslims, Usama the man of letters was the one worth remembering. His companion 'Imad al-Din said that "Usama was, in the power of his poetry and prose, like his name ('lion')." His former pupil Ibn 'Asakir of Damascus shared a fellow's florid assessment (Ibn 'Asakir, *Ta'rikh*, 1998, 8:90–91):

The amir Usama was one of the poets of the age, holding the reins of poetry and prose ... He cannot be described by one sole quality, nor can one explicate his poetry by the tongue alone. His lengthy odes are almost indistinguishable from those of [the great Arab poet] Ibn al-Walid, nor would it be denied if they were attributed to [the great poet] Labid. They come as if from the tip of his tongue thanks to the clarity of his expression; they are not overly long, nor does his elevated style become mixed up in useless digression ... in every one is a rare meaning and a delightful resonance.

Derenbourg may have been so quick to call Usama a hero because it was he who was first to rediscover, edit, and translate Usama's "memoirs," the *Book of Learning by Example*. For modern readers, that book, more than any other, has immortalized Usama, if only among students of Islamic history, Arabic literature, and the Crusades. "If any book is the man, [the *Book of Learning by Example*] is certainly Usama," as Hitti, Usama's most venerated English translator, put it. In a way, such a close identification of a man with one book is a pity, for it has overshadowed Usama's other literary achievements, particularly his poetic anthologies and works of criticism. Through a combination of modern academic trends and the sheer serendipity of manuscript discoveries, Usama's "memoirs" have tended to over-shadow his poetic achievements, making his medieval reputation as a poet of the age seem undeserved. But, with almost all his surviving works now in edited form, we are in a better position to appreciate more fully Usama and his works.

Usama did his best to portray himself as an attractive personality, and so it is easy to see how, for Derenbourg and others, he might fit into a familiar heroic mould. His youth was full of promise, and his life full of movement and some genuine literary achievements. But he was also vain, ambitious, and probably a bit of a liar. If we only knew Usama at age thirty or so, we might find him to be as odious as did his uncle Sultan. But modern readers find Usama at the end of his story, when he has lived a long and fascinating life. Part of his appeal is that he shares so much of this life with us in his autobiographical writings, asking us to sit down with him as he recounts his tales of lions and amirs. The obnoxious younger Usama, by the time we get to him, has had some of his preciousness kicked out. He appears more human and fragile than that younger hero, more accessible. An aging knight of sorrowful countenance pestering Saladin with fulsome poetry and dreamy old war stories, he calls forth no one so much as Don Quixote, and we readers become his unwitting Sancho Panza.

For this biographer, Usama stands out above all as a uniquely knowable medieval human being, a human granted the gift of literary style, but, even so, a mere mortal. At the end of his long life, Usama was a maker of the Muslim world in the way that many unheroic humans, in small and humble ways, contribute to the fabric of their worlds. The contribution of Usama ibn Munqidh to the Muslim world was not forged in battle nor settled in the palace, but inked on the page. His political fortunes varied and were often grim, but Usama's poetry and mastery of the glories of his language found him a place among his peers; his love of autobiographical reflection has made him equally beloved by his modern readers. It is thus not in his victories or intrigues where Usama shines as a maker, but in his writing – in subtle meanderings into love and sadness and in playful twists of mode and meaning, a rare and memorable human voice.

FURTHER READING

GENERAL

Much of the scholarship relating to Usama and his world is written in languages other than English, especially in French and Arabic, and so the English-language suggestions here are only the beginning. No better introduction to Usama and his world can be had than his own reminiscences: fortunately, his *Book of Learning by Example* has been translated into just about every major European language, including English. The currently favored translation is that of Philip K. Hitti, *An Arab-Syrian Gentleman and Warrior in the Period of the Crusades* (New York: Columbia University Press, 1929 [repr. 2000]). The autobiographical anecdotes in his other works have also been translated. See Paul M. Cobb, "Usama ibn Munqidh's *Book of the Staff (Kitab al-'Asa)*: Autobiographical and Historical Excerpts," *Al-Masaq: Islam and the Medieval Mediterranean* 17 (2005): 109–123; and idem, "Usama ibn Munqidh's *Kernels of Refinement (Lubab al-Adab)*: Autobiographical and Historical Excerpts," *Al-Masaq: Islam and the Medieval Mediterranean* 18 (2006): forthcoming.

The pioneering biographical treatment of Usama by Derenbourg is still a mine of information for those who read French: Hartwig Derenbourg, *Ousâma ibn Mounkidh. Un emir syrien au premier siècle des croisades (1095–1188). Tome Premier: Vie d'Ousâma* (Paris: Ernest Leroux, 1889). With regard to Usama's literary output, especially in poetry, Derenbourg's study has been superseded by a massive study in Arabic by Hasan 'Abbas, *Usama ibn Munqidh: Hayatuhu wa-Atharuhu*, 2 vols. (Cairo: al-Hay'a al-Misriya al-'Ama li'l-Kitab, 1981).

For a concise general survey of the period of the Crusades from the perspective of Christendom, see Jonathan Riley-Smith, *The Crusades: A Short History*, 2nd ed. (New Haven: Yale University Press, 2005), with a guide to the major scholarly studies; for Muslim perspectives, Carole Hillenbrand, *The Crusades: Islamic Perspectives* (New York: Routledge, 2000) is hard to beat.

A good, but weighty, general survey of Islamic history can be had in Ira Lapidus, *A History of Islamic Societies*, 2nd ed., (Cambridge: Cambridge University Press, 2002). The religion of Islam in the medieval period can be surveyed in Jonathan Berkey, *The Formation of Islam: Religion and Society in the Near East, 600–1800* (Cambridge: Cambridge University Press, 2003). The glories of Arabic literature are analyzed to death in the various volumes of the *Cambridge History of Arabic Literature*, but no volume covering Usama's period has emerged. Readers will be doing themselves a favor by sampling the literature in translation. Robert Irwin's modern-day *adab* anthology *Night and Horses and the Desert* (Woodstock: Overlook Press, 2000) is as fine a sample of Usama's literary world as one could wish. Two standard scholarly references on Islamic matters deserve mention, too: the *Encyclopaedia of Islam*, 2nd ed. (Leiden, 1954–2001) and the *Encyclopaedia of the Qur'an* (Leiden, 2001 – in progress).

CHAPTER 1

Shayzar itself has not yet received a full-length study, but an Italian archaeological team headed by Cristina Tonghini is currently investigating the site. For a survey of Crusader-era castles, Frankish and Muslim, Hugh Kennedy, *Crusader Castles* (Cambridge: Cambridge University Press, 1994), is a lovely place to start. A social history of children in medieval Islam has yet to be written, but a very intriguing study of medieval Islamic concepts of childhood is Avner Giladi, *Children of Islam* (New York: St. Martin's Press, 1992). On hunting and falconry, in English, there is only Zaki Hasan's *Hunting as Practised in Arab Countries of the Middle Ages* (Cairo, 1937), and the anonymous treatise translated by Terence Clark and Muawiya Derhalli as *Al-Mansur's Book on Hunting* (Warminster, 2001).

CHAPTER 2

For the political history of the reigns of Usama's various patrons, the reader will be well served by P. M. Holt, *The Age of the Crusades* (London: Longman, 1986), and the relevant chapters on the Fatimids, Ayyubids and Crusaders by Paul Walker, Paula Sanders, and Michael Chamberlain in Carl F. Petry, ed., *The Cambridge History of Egypt, Volume One* (Cambridge: Cambridge University Press, 1998).

CHAPTER 3

On aspects of Usama's literary *oeuvre*, see David Morray, *The Genius of Usama ibn Munqidh* (Durham, 1987) and Robert Irwin, "Usamah ibn Munqidh: An Arab-Syrian Gentleman at the Time of the Crusades Reconsidered," in J. France and W. G. Zajac, eds., *The Crusades and Their Sources. Essays Presented to Bernard Hamilton* (Aldershot, 1998), 71–87.

CHAPTER 4

On Islam and its practice as Usama knew it, see Berkey, *Formation*, and Josef W. Meri, *The Cult of Saints among Muslims and Jews in medieval Syria* (Oxford: Oxford University Press, 2002). On women, see Leila Ahmed, *Women and Gender in Islam* (New Haven: Yale University Press, 1992). Medieval concepts of masculinity await a study. For now see the studies on modern concepts, some of them indebted to medieval ideas, in Mai Ghoussoub and Emma Sinclair-Webb, eds., *Imagined Masculinities: Male Identity and Culture in the Modern Middle East* (London: Saqi Books, 2000). On Islamic attitudes towards animals, see now Richard C. Foltz, *Animals in Islamic Tradition and Muslim Cultures* (Oxford: Oneworld Publications, 2005).

CHAPTER 5

On Muslim views of the Franks, Hillenbrand, *Islamic Perspectives*, is fundamental (and the source of much of the material in this chapter). On the principality of Antioch, see Thomas S. Asbridge, *The Creation of the Principality of Antioch, 1098–1130* (Woodbridge: Boydell Press, 2000). On Frankish and Islamic medicine, see Piers D. Mitchell, *Medicine in the Crusades* (Cambridge: Cambridge University Press, 2004) and, with special reference to Usama, Lawrence I. Conrad, "Usama ibn Munqidh and Other Witnesses to Frankish and Islamic Medicine in the Era of the Crusades," in Zohar Amar et al., eds., *Medicine in Jerusalem throughout the Ages* (Tel Aviv: C. G. Foundation, 1999), pp. xxvi–lii. Islamic law awaits its great synthesis. But see the older pioneering work of Joseph Schacht, *An Introduction to Islamic Law* (Oxford: Clarendon Press, 1964). On trial by ordeal, see Robert Bartlett, *Trial by Fire and Water: The Medieval Judicial Ordeal* (Oxford: Clarendon Press, 1986). On Islamic views of Christians and Christianity, see Hillenbrand, *Islamic Perspectives*, pp. 303 ff.

WORKS CITED

'Abbas, Hasan. 1981. *Usama ibn Munqidh: Hayatuhu wa-Atharuhu*. Cairo: al-Hay'a al-Misriya al-'Ama li'l-Kitab.

Abu Shama. 1997. *Kitab al-Rawdatayn fi Akhbar al-Dawlatayn*. Edited by Ibrahim Zaybaq. Beirut: Mu'assasat al-Risala.

Barhebraeus. 2004. *Butyrum Sapientiae*. Edited and translated by N. Peter Joosse as *A Syriac Encyclopaedia of Aristotelian Philosophy*. Leiden: Brill.

Derenbourg, Hartwig. 1889. *Ousâma ibn Mounkidh. Un emir syrien au premier siècle des croisades (1095–1188). Tome Premier: Vie d'Ousâma*. Paris: Ernest Leroux.

Fulcher of Chartres. 1913. *Fulcheri Cartonensis Historia Hierosolymitana (1095–1127)*. Heidelberg: Carl Winters Universitätsbuchhandlung. Translated by Frances Rita Ryan as *A History of the Expedition to Jerusalem*. Knoxville: The University of Tennessee Press, 1969.

Hillenbrand, Carole. 2000. *The Crusades. Islamic Perspectives*. London and New York: Routledge.

Ibn al-'Adim, Kamal al-Din 'Umar. 1968. *Zubdat al-Halab min Ta'rikh Halab*. Edited by Sami Dahhan. Damascus: Institut Français de Damas.
– 1988. *Bughyat al-Talab fi Ta'rikh Halab*. Edited by Suhayl Zakkar. Damascus: n.p.

Ibn 'Asakir, Abu al-Qasim 'Ali. 1998. *Ta'rikh Madinat Dimashq*. Edited by 'Umar al-'Amrawi. Beirut: Dar al-Fikr.

Ibn al-Athir, Abu al-Hasan 'Ali. 1966. *Al-Kamil fi al-Ta'rikh*. Beirut: Dar Sadir.

Ibn Khallikan, Shams al-Din Ahmad. 1968. *Wafayat al-A'yan wa-Anba' Abna' al-Zaman*. Edited by Ihsan 'Abbas. Beirut: Dar Sadir.

Ibn al-Qalanisi, Abu Ya'la Hamza. 1983. *Ta'rikh Dimashq*. Edited by Suhayl Zakkar. Damascus: Dar Hassan.

'Imad al-Din al-Isfahani. 1951. *Kharidat al-Qasr wa-Jaridat al-'Asr. (Al-Sham)*. Edited by Shukri Faysal. Damascus: n.p.

Peter Tudebode. 1977. *Historia de Hierosolymitana Itinere*. Edited by J. and L. Hill. Paris: Librairie Orientaliste Paul Guenther. Translated by J. and L. Hill. Philadelphia: American Philosophical Society, 1974.

Peters, Edward, ed. 1998. *The First Crusade. The Chronicle of Fulcher of Chartres and Other Source Materials*. 2nd ed. Philadelphia: University of Pennsylvania Press.

Usama ibn Munqidh. 1930. *Kitab al-I'tibar*. Edited by Philip K. Hitti. Princeton: Princeton University Press. Translated by Philip K. Hitti as *An Arab-Syrian Gentleman and Warrior in the Period of the Crusades*. New York: Columbia University Press, 1929.

— 1935. *Lubab al-Adab*. Edited by A. M. Shakir. Cairo: Maktabat Luwis Sarkis. Partial translation by Paul M. Cobb as "Usama ibn Munqidh's *Kernels of Refinement (Lubab al-Adab)*: Autobiographical and Historical Excerpts." *Al-Masaq: Islam and the Medieval Mediterranean* 18 (2006): forthcoming.

— 1953. *Diwan Usama ibn Munqidh*. Edited by A. Badawi and H. 'Abd al-Majid. Cairo: Wizarat al-Ma'arif al-'Umumiyya.

— 1968. *Kitab al-Manazil wa'l-Diyar*. Edited by M. Hijazi. Cairo: Al-Majlis al-A'la li-al-Shu'un al-Islamiyya.

— 1978. *Kitab al-'Asa*. Edited by Hasan 'Abbas. Alexandria: Al-Hay'at al-Misriyya al-'Amma li-al-Kitab. Partial translation by Paul M. Cobb as "Usama ibn Munqidh's *Book of the Staff (Kitab al-'Asa)*: Autobiographical and Historical Excerpts." *Al-Masaq: Islam and the Medieval Mediterranean* 17 (2005): 109–123.

— 1987. *Al-Badi' fi'l-badi'*. Edited by A. Muhanna. Beirut: Dar al-Kutub al-'Ilmiyya.

— n.d. Manaqib 'Umar ibn al-Khattab wa-Manaqib 'Umar ibn 'Abd al-'Aziz, Dar al-Kutub, Cairo: MS *ta'rikh* Taymur #1513 (11147).

William of Tyre. 1986. *Chronicon*. Edited by R. B. C. Huygens. Turnhout: Brepols. Translated by Emily Babcock and August Krey as *A History of Deeds Done Beyond the Sea*. New York: Columbia University Press, 1943.

PRINCIPAL PEOPLE
ENCOUNTERED IN THIS BOOK

Al-'Abbas Stepson of Ibn al-Sallar. Fatimid commander who, after Ibn al-Sallar's death, was made vizier. He died in a skirmish with the Franks while fleeing Egypt with Usama in 1154.

Abu 'Abdallah Usama's tutor, a great grammarian and native of Toledo, Spain.

'Ali Usama's brother. A great warrior and ascetic. He died in battle against the Franks at Ascalon in 1151 or 1152. Also the name of a kinsman of the Prophet Muhammad, considered the first Shi'ite imam and, for Sunnis, the fourth of the "Rightly Guided" caliphs.

Al-Hafiz Fatimid caliph, 1131–1149.

Ibn Mula'ib Local Syrian warlord and bandit chief. His headquarters were for a time at the town of Apamea near Shayzar. Killed in 1106 by Nizaris.

Ibn Munira Usama's tutor, a poet and man of letters from the Syrian town of Kafartab. Died 1158.

Ibn Ruzzik Fatimid commander and vizier in the wake of the failure of al-'Abbas. A companion of Usama, he sought to have him return to Egypt after he fled to the court of Nur al-Din. He died in 1161.

Ibn al-Sallar Fatimid vizier under the title "al-'Adil," after forcing the caliph al-Zafir to name him to the position. He was assassinated in 1153.

Mahmud Burid prince of Damascus, and nominal servant of the Saljuq sultan. He died in 1139.

Muhammad There were three Muhammads of great importance to Usama.

1) The Prophet of Islam and God's Messenger, who founded the first Muslim state in Arabia. He died in 632;

2) Usama's brother, who accompanied him to Egypt, captured by the Franks when Usama was forced to flee Egypt, but eventually ransomed;

3) Usama's cousin, the son of his uncle Sultan and the last lord of Shayzar. These last two died in the earthquake at Shayzar in 1157.

Murhaf The son of Usama and later an amir and close companion of Saladin. Died 1216 or 1217.

Murshid Usama's father. Died 1136.

Nasr Son of al-'Abbas and assassin of Ibn al-Sallar. He was captured by the Franks while fleeing Egypt with Usama and later executed in 1154.

Nur al-Din Son and successor of Zangi, he added Damascus to the domains of his father and ruled there. Usama worked in his service after fleeing from Egypt. Died in 1174.

Qara Arslan Artuqid lord of Diyar Bakr, based at Hisn Kayfa. Usama's patron in his later years. He died in 1167.

Ridwan Former Fatimid vizier under the title al-Malik al-Afdal, he was forced to flee Egypt after the caliph connived against him. Usama tried to convince him to assist the Burids of Damascus against Zangi, but Ridwan became involved in a plot in Egypt and was killed there. He died in 1144.

Saladin Commander for Nur al-Din, founder of the Ayyubid dynasty of Egypt, Syria, and Yemen, and reconqueror of Jerusalem. Usama's last patron, he died in Damascus in 1193.

Sultan ibn 'Ali Usama's uncle and lord of Shayzar. Died 1154.

Unur Burid commander-in-chief and atabeg of the Burid princes of Damascus, bearing the title "Mu'in al-Din." Patron of Usama. He died in 1149.

Usama ibn Munqidh The subject of this biography. Died 1188.

Al-Yaghisiyani A commander and governor of the city of Hama for Zangi. He was Usama's immediate superior when working for Zangi. He died in 1157.

Al-Zafir Fatimid caliph, 1149–1154.

Zangi Atabeg of Mosul, conqueror of Crusader Edessa, and lord of a dominion that included northern Iraq and northern Syria. Usama worked in his service in his early days. He died in 1146.

SIMPLIFIED LISTS OF PRINCIPAL DYNASTIES AND RULERS IN USAMA'S LIFETIME

1 ISLAMIC POLITIES

The Banu Munqidh of Shayzar:

1081–1082: Sadid al-Mulk 'Ali ibn Munqidh

1082–1098: 'Izz al-Dawla Nasr

1098–1154: 'Izz al-Din Sultan

1154–1157: Taj al-Dawla Muhammad

Lords of Aleppo:

Saljuq princes:

1095–1113: Ridwan

1113: Alp Arslan al-Akhras

1114–1123: Sultan Shah

Artuqid amirs:

1120–1122: Ilghazi ibn Artuq

1122–1123: Badr al-Dawla Sulayman

1123–1124: Nur al-Dawla Balak

1124–1125: Husam al-Din Timurtash

1125–1126: Aq Sunqur al-Bursuqi

1126: Mas'ud ibn Aq Sunqur

Interregnum and Zangid conquest

1128–1147: Zangi, atabeg of Mosul and Aleppo

1147–1174: Nur al-Din Mahmud

1174–1181: al-Salih Isma'il

Interregnum and Ayyubid conquest

1183–1216: al-Zahir Ghazi

Lords of Damascus:

Saljuq princes:

1095–1104: Duqaq

1104: Tutush II

Burid amirs:

    1104–1128: Tughtakin, atabeg of Damascus

    1128–1132:Buri ibn Tughtakin

    1132–1135: Isma'il ibn Buri

    1135–1139: Mahmud ibn Buri

    1139–1140: Muhammad ibn Buri

    1140–1154: Abaq ibn Muhammad

Zangid amirs:

    1154–1174: Nur al-Din Mahmud

    1174: Al-Salih Isma'il

Ayyubid conquest

    1174–1193: Salah al-Din Yusuf (Saladin)

Lords of Hisn Kayfa:

    1102–1109: Sökmen I ibn Artuq

    1109–1144: Dawud ibn Sökmen

    1144–1167: Qara Arslan ibn Dawud

    1167–1185: Muhammad ibn Qara Arslan

    1185–1201: Sökmen II ibn Muhammad

The Fatimid caliphs of Egypt and Syria:

    1094–1101: Al-Musta'li

    1101–1130: Al-Amir

    1130–1131: Interregnum (Al-Hafiz as regent)

    1131–1149: Al-Hafiz

    1149–1154: Al-Zafir

    1154–1160: Al-Fa'iz

    1160–1171: Al-'Adid

    1171: Caliphate dissolved by Saladin

The Abbasid Caliphs of Baghdad:

    1094–1118: Al-Mustazhir

    1118–1135: Al-Mustarshid

    1135–1136: Al-Rashid

    1136–1160: Al-Mustanjid

    1160–1170: Al-Mustadi'

    1170–1180: Al-Nasir

1180–1225: Al-Zahir

The Saljuq sultans in Iran and Iraq:
1094–1105: Barkiyaruq
1105: Malik Shah II
1105–1118: Muhammad I Tapar
1118–1157: Ahmad Sanjar

In Iraq & western Iran only:
1118–1131: Mahmud II
1131–1132: Dawud
1132–1134: Toghril II
1134–1152: Mas'ud
1152–1153: Malik Shah III
1153–1159: Muhammad II
1160–1161: Sulayman Shah
1161–1176: Arslan Shah
1176–1194: Toghril III

2 FRANKISH POLITIES

The Principality of Antioch:
1099–1104: Bohemond of Taranto
1104–1112: Tancred (regent)
1112–1119: Roger of Salerno (regent)
1119–1126: Baldwin II of Le Bourcq (regent)
1126–1130: Bohemond II
1130–1136: Jerusalem regency (Baldwin II, Fulk of Anjou)
1136–1149: Constance of Antioch (w/Raymond of Poitiers)
1149–1153: Constance of Antioch (alone)
1153–1160: Constance of Antioch (w/Reynald of Châtillon)
1160–1163: Constance of Antioch (alone)
1163–1201: Bohemond III

The Kingdom of Jerusalem:
1099–1100: Godfrey of Bouillon
1100–1118: Baldwin I of Boulogne
1118–1131: Baldwin II of Le Bourcq
1131–1143: Melisende of Jerusalem (w/Fulk of Anjou)
1143–1163: Baldwin III (w/Melisende as co-monarch until 1152)
1163–1174: Amalric

1174–1185: Baldwin IV
1185–1186: Baldwin V
1186–1190: Guy of Lusignan

INDEX